ZERO-RESISTANCE
RESISTANCE
SELLING

Other Books by Dr. Maxwell Maltz

Psycho-Cybernetics, published by Pocket Books.

Psycho-Cybernetics 2000 (by Dr. Maltz and Dr. Bobbe Sommer), published by Prentice Hall.

The Magic Power of Self-Image, published by The Psycho-Cybernetics Foundation, Inc.

Search for Self-Respect in a Disrespectful World, published by The Psycho-Cybernetics Foundation, Inc.

ZERO-RESISTANCE SELLING

Maxwell Maltz, M.D., F.I.C.S.
with **Dan S. Kennedy, William T. Brooks, Matt Oechsli, Jeff Paul and Pamela Yellen**

PRENTICE HALL PRESS

PRENTICE HALL PRESS
A member of Penguin Putnam Inc.
375 Hudson Street
New York, N.Y. 10014
www.penguinputnam.com

Library of Congress Cataloging-in-Publication Data

Maltz, Maxwell
Zero-resistance selling / Maxwell Maltz ; with Dan S. Kennedy . . . [et al.].
    p.   cm.
ISBN 0-13-609074-5 (cloth)   ISBN 0-7352-0039-4 (paper)
1. Selling.   2. Success in business.   I. Kennedy, Dan S.   II. Title.
HF5438.25.M327   1997
658.85—dc21   97-28993   CIP

Printed in the United States of America

10   9   8   7   6   5   4   3   2   1   20 19 18 17 16 15 14 13 12 11

About the Authors

William Brooks is the CEO of The Brooks Group, a leading developer and provider of sophisticated sales training programs to corporations of all types and sizes. Bill is a former successful college football coach, has served as CEO of a 300-million dollar organization with over 4,000 sales representatives, and, in 18 years, he has presented more than 2,500 speeches and seminars to companies like General Motors, Hewlett-Packard, Mack Trucks and Home Depot. He is the author of five books, including *You're Working Too Hard to Make the Sale.* Bill is a Founding Member of the Board of Directors of The Psycho-Cybernetics Foundation, Inc. For a copy of his free report "The 21 Biggest Myths in Sales & How to Destroy Them," call, fax or write: The Brooks Group, 1903 Ashwood Court, #C, Greensboro, NC 27455, Fax (910) 282-5707, Phone (800) 633-7762.

Dan S. Kennedy is an entrepreneur, in-demand direct marketing consultant, sales trainer and professional speaker. Dan speaks to more than 200,000 people a year, frequently appearing on public seminar programs with other business speakers like Zig Ziglar, Tom Hopkins and Jim Rohn, dignitaries like President Bush, General Norman Schwarzkopf and William Bennett, Olympians Mary Lou Retton and Bonnie Blair, coaches and sports stars like Jimmy Johnson, Lou Holtz, Troy Aikman and Mike Singletarry, even entertainers like Bill Cosby. Dan is the prolific author of six books, including *How to Make Millions with Your Ideas.* He is a Founding Member of the Board of Directors and President of the Psycho-Cybernetics Foundation. For a free copy of Dan's book, tape and tool kit catalog and other information, write or Fax: Dan Kennedy, 5818 N. 7th Street #103, Phoenix, AZ 85014, Fax (602) 269-3113.

Matt Oechsli holds an MBA in marketing and has successfully combined his background in sales and marketing with work in therapeutic hypnosis and professional counseling. His corporate clients include virtually every major firm in financial services: Merrill Lynch, Prudential, Paine Webber, etc. Matt has been featured in articles in *Fortune* magazine, *Inc.* and *The Wall Street Journal*. He is the author of several books, including *Winning the Inner Game of Selling*, and *The Performance Revolution System of Selling* used by many major corporations. Matt is a Founding Member of the Board of Directors of the Psycho-Cybernetics Foundation, Inc. For free information about his publications, products and services, write, fax or call: The Oechsli Institute, 2102 N. Elm, Greensboro, NC 27408; Phone (910) 273-6582, Fax (910) 273-2342.

Jeff Paul, Certified Financial Planner, is the owner of several publishing businesses and, in recent years, has provided in-depth training in "Emotional Marketing" to 12,400 sales professionals. He is the author of several sales courses, including "101 Secrets to a 6-Figure Income" and "Insider Secrets of Running a Million-Dollar Practice." He also writes several specialized newsletters which are read by more than 15,000 sales professionals each month. His nationally advertised book *How To Make $4,000 a Day Sitting at Your Kitchen Table in Your Underwear* (about the mail-order business) has sold over 70,000 copies. Jeff is a founding member of the Board of Directors of the Psycho-Cybernetics Foundation. For free information about his books, courses and services, write, fax or call: Profit Planning System 1811 W. Diehl Road, #600, Naperville, IL 60563; Phone: (708) 778-9996, FAX: (708) 778-9927.

Pamela Yellen is CEO of the Prospecting and Marketing Institute, Inc. Founded in 1990, the company specializes in helping sales professionals and entire sales and service organizations dramatically improve profits. She was educated at the Universities of South Florida and San Francisco, where she received a degree in Psychology. She has spoken to more than 1,000 groups throughout the world. Pamela has also authored numerous audio- and video-training programs, and is codeveloper, with Dan Kennedy, of the "Magnetic Recruiting System" which has revolutionized the way the insurance industry attracts and recruits new agents. For a free copy of Pamela's report: "Seven Secrets of Successful Prospecting," call (800) 927-9410 or (505) 466-1167, or write 39 Vista Estrella South, Lamy, NM 87540.

About the Psycho-Cybernetics Foundation, Inc.

The Psycho-Cybernetics Foundation, Inc. is dedicated to creating a new "renaissance" in self-image psychology, by making all the works of Dr. Maxwell Maltz available, as well as developing new publications with Dr. Maltz as co-author along with contemporary authors, speakers and other leaders in the human potential field. The Foundation is engaged in publishing partnerships with a number of major corporations, including Simon & Schuster, Prentice Hall, Pocket Books, and Audio Renaissance.

The foundation's founding Board of Directors is made up of four of America's most respected and successful business educators and self-improvement authors. The foundation directs a portion of its profits to free distribution of Dr. Maltz's works to prisons and schools that have been nominated by our members.

The foundation also publishes "The Zero-Resistance Letter," conducts seminars and conferences, and licenses the use of Dr. Maltz' materials to selected experts in specialized fields.

Preface

One of the Most Unusual Books Ever Written

Dr. Maxwell Maltz passed away in 1975, yet he is the primary author of this book written in 1996, and he contributed in a very active and lively way. You undoubtedly know of Dr. Maltz's book *Psycho-Cybernetics*, first published in 1960 and never off the bookstore shelves for a day since. What you may not know is that Dr. Maltz was a remarkably prolific researcher and writer, so that by the time of his death, he had recorded over a dozen books and three complete courses of study on Psycho-Cybernetics, never published, advanced material on Zero-Resistance Living and Zero-Resistance Selling, and thousands of pages of research and counseling session notes. All of this material was put into a computer, carefully sorted and organized, so that Dr. Maltz could continue contributing to new works even today.

Five other top, contemporary authors, all experts on selling and on Psycho-Cybernetics, joined with Dr. Maltz (via the computer) to write this book: Pamela Yellen, Bill Brooks, Matthew Oechsli, Jeff Paul, and Dan Kennedy. These five authors have merged their voices with Dr. Maltz. To prevent confusion and clutter, you are hearing everything spoken by one voice, but you should know it is really five voices merged and melded together. Five collections of life experiences, five experts in applied Psycho-Cybernetics. Five coaches and consultants to peak performers. In a sense, five for the price of one!

The book is in one voice, Dr. Maltz's voice, and reads as if Dr. Maltz wrote it today. We know he would be proud of this work and we know that you will benefit from it enormously.

Contents

Introduction

"Once Difficult, Now Easy"—This is the battle cry of applied Creative Psycho-Cybernetics. You have undoubtedly acquired this book for one of two reasons: one, some aspect of selling is or has become difficult for you, in which case we guarantee it will be transformed to "easy!" by the time you finish; or two, you are doing very well but are looking for a little edge, a way to do even a bit better. You will be rewarded as you read on.

Over 30 million copies of Dr. Maltz's first book, *Psycho-Cybernetics*, have been sold worldwide, a great many to sales professionals, mostly at the urging of their sales managers, peers, or friends. In *Zero-Resistance Selling*, Dr. Maltz's most powerful methods are directed specifically and exclusively at the selling experience, with the objective of wiping away all resistance that occurs between prospect and salesperson and within the salesperson himself.

There are a few "basics" of Psycho-Cybernetics you will need to be familiar with before we begin:

Self-Image

While in practice as a plastic surgeon, Dr. Maltz encountered many people who exaggerated their physical problems far beyond reality, like a man with slightly oversized ears who insisted he had "giant elephant ears" which prevented anybody from taking him seriously, so he could not get ahead in life. Dr. Maltz also worked with patients who insisted they saw little difference in their reflection in the mirror, even after surgery had actually made miraculous changes.

Dr. Maltz became increasingly convinced that people often had an inner image of themselves damaged by emotional scars. Through extensive research, counseling with hundreds of patients, and his own remarkable insights, Dr. Maltz developed a unique understanding of this inner image and how it sets up and enforces the parameters of achievement and happiness for each individual. The self-image is held in the subconscious mind and becomes a composite of everything you've ever been told, read, learned, or experienced about yourself. In a way, it is your opinion of yourself, and it literally sets the limits of what you can and cannot accomplish.

From birth on, your authority figures—parents, grandparents, teachers, even peers—are busy "programming" your self-image, telling it things about you and your relationship to the world that may or may not be accurate, may or may not remain accurate as you mature, and may or may not be helpful. For example, the "Don't Talk to Strangers" may be very useful for a five-year-old boy, but not for a 35-year-old salesman! The programming that is repeated most frequently and forcefully, and is reinforced by experience, becomes like the grooves etched into a record or, to stick with the computer analogy, the system installed on your hard drive.

The good news is that it can be "re-programmed" in a very deliberate, goal-directed manner. In this book, you will discover how your self-image may help, but probably also hinders your success in selling, and how to liberate your self image from inaccurate programming.

Servo-Mechanism

This is the core of Psycho-Cybernetics. Dr. Maltz determined that the subconscious mind has within it an awesomely powerful Servo (servant) Mechanism, controlled by the self-image, that works tirelessly to guide you to whatever objectives it is clearly given, much like the guided-missile technology. The Servo-Mechanism has a split personality; it can be either an Automatic Success Mechanism or an Automatic Failure Mechanism, depending on what is asked of it and what is communicated to it through the self-image. The mechanism has no built-in bias in one direction or the other. In this book, you will learn how to communicate with this Servo-Mechanism so it operates as an Automatic Success Mechanism.

Mental Rehearsal

Dr. Maltz developed a concept called "Theater of Your Mind," to facilitate effective, vivid mental rehearsal. Today, more than 30 years after he wrote *Psycho-Cybernetics*, his ideas about mental rehearsal have become the basis for the booming field of sports psychology. The same mental rehearsal strategies that help athletes excel and perform well under pressure can give your selling career a giant boost. Mental rehearsal is especially important because the self-image cannot differentiate between real and synthetic (vividly, repetitively imagined) experience, so this is one of the best ways to reprogram the self-image.

You'll become more comfortable with these terms and concepts as you proceed through this book. For a complete understanding, you will probably also want to read the original *Psycho-Cybernetics* and *Psycho-Cybernetics 2000*, both readily available in bookstores. Or, for a complete catalog of available books and cassettes, you can contact The Psycho-Cybernetics Foundation at (602) 265-1922 or fax (602) 269-3113.

The goal of this book—Zero-Resistance Selling—means a new kind of selling experience, free of all the resistance and obstacles manufactured inside the mind, *and* free of the resistance served up by prospects who sense insecurity on the part of the salesperson. Get a picture in your mind of going to the refrigerator and taking out a stick of butter, to put on a piece of bread. The butter is hard as a rock from being refrigerated. If you use an ordinary knife taken out of the drawer, you'll have to push hard, probably saw back and forth, just to chip a pad of butter off the whole stick. Then spreading it will be a problem, too.

But picture yourself with a heated butter knife in hand. Armed with that warmed knife, you slice through that cold, hard stick of butter effortlessly. Armed with the understanding of your own self-image and the Creative Psycho-Cybernetic Techniques in this book, you will soon slice through *all* resistance effortlessly. Anything that has been difficult for you will become easy! You will become the effective salesperson you've always wanted to be.

Dan S. Kennedy
President, The Psycho-Cybernetics Foundation, Inc.

Chapter 1

How to Conquer Call Reluctance

What is call reluctance? *It is best typified by the salesperson who hangs around the office every morning drinking coffee and chewing the fat with other salespeople rather than getting out into the field for the earliest possible start; the sales pro who shuffles paper rather than dials the phone numbers of his prospects. The one who procrastinates all day long by rationalizing:*

> "It's just barely 9:00. That's not a good time to call anybody. They've just barely settled in. Still grumpy about the commuter traffic. I'll wait a little while."

> "It's 10:00. Most of my prospects are really busy right now with morning meetings, getting their staff squared away. The morning mail's arriving. It'll be best to let them get past this really busy time before I call and interrupt them."

> "It's 11:00 already. Where does the darn day go? A lot of people start going out to lunch at 11:00. I'll wind up leaving messages all over the place. I'll wait until after lunch hour to make these calls."

> "It's 1:30. Everybody ought to be back from lunch. But they have calls to return. People waiting for them. I'd better give them a few minutes to get settled.

"Look at that—it's 3:30 already! You can't call executives now. They're all wrapping up the day, to get an early start on the afternoon traffic. Guess I'll just get organized for an early start tomorrow morning. That's the ticket—I'll get after 'em bright and early tomorrow."

Perhaps it's the sales pro who dials and thinks "hope he's not there, hope he's not there, hope he's not there" or drops in and, when told his prospect cannot see him today, actually feels a comforting wave of relief wash over. Is this you?

If it is not you all the time, it probably *is* you some of the time. Because fears, doubts, and anxieties are the plagues that infect most sales professionals, preventing them from peak achievements, maximum earnings, and great enjoyment. Avoidance of the possibilities of rejection and failure is the disease rampant in the ranks of sales professionals.

Call reluctance, procrastination, avoidance, describe it as you wish, but it is all symptomatic of inner turmoil rather than inner calm; of insecurity rather than confidence; of an "argument" between your aspirations, intentions and true self-image.

One thing is certain: the key to taking your sales performance and results to the next level is not to be found in some new "technique." Nor can it be produced from willpower, determination, or dogged persistence. This key can only be found inside, not outside. And that is what Creative Psycho-Cybernetics is all about; finding and using that key, with the result of making what has been difficult for you in selling suddenly easy.

I am going to tell you some truths about yourself in this chapter, and throughout this book, that you may not like to hear. You may want to argue them, but you cannot profit by doing so. You can only gain by carefully considering these ideas, testing them, trying them, and seeing whether or not they have an impact on you. You see yourself now through a distorted mirror. Your ego tries to wheel a mirror in front of you that distorts and conceals truths about your behavior, so that you can deny responsibility and place the blame for all unsatisfactory results somewhere else. That is the ego's mission.

Your self-image provides a different mirror, but it, too, is distorted by all kinds of past conditioning, erroneous input from others, outdated information and unchallenged habits. Its mission is to safeguard you from pain by keeping you within your limits.

We must break through these distortions to find the truth, free the self-image, and literally alter our core beliefs if we are to alter our life experiences for the better.

How the Self-Image Controls What You Can and Cannot Do in Selling

Why does a sales pro begin the day, showering and getting dressed, with the very best of intentions about making lots of calls, but then fritter away the day doing everything *but* making those calls?

A warning before the answer: this is a vicious, self-sabotaging behavior, because it validates your worst beliefs about yourself. After a day like that, your self-image says: "See, I told you so." The more that happens, the harder it is to free the self-image from the belief that you are just not going to make those kinds of calls. The more you avoid, the harder it is to confront. The habit of avoidance is one of the hardest of all habits to break.

Back to the question of "why." Simply put, the self-image is a complex collection of beliefs about you, compiled from many different sources over a period of years. It defines your possibilities, and limits what you can and cannot do. As a very simple example of this in action, consider the 40-year-old, reasonably successful, handsome and articulate man who quakes with fear and turns to mush at the thought of asking an attractive woman out on a date. There is no legitimate physical reason for this failure behavior. He has no speech impediments, he has no physical deformity, he does not suffer from halitosis, nor is he mentally handicapped. In other situations, he is smart, witty, confident. So why is he blocked from successful performance in this particular situation? Why does he feel zero resistance when, say, asking a co-worker for a favor or asserting his opinions in a meeting, but overwhelmed by resistance at the moment of asking a woman out to dinner and the theater? If you can understand the "why" about this peculiar, self-defeating behavior, you can also discover the great truth behind all such behavior, including your own.

Without questioning this man at length, I cannot tell you for certain the specifics of how his self-image has been programmed to cause his confidence to collapse, glands perspire feverishly, palms dampen, and tongue turn to mush in this situation. But I can give you a very good example of how this has occurred. In fact, I will tell you about an actual man, a business executive I'll call John G. who exhibited this exact behavior.

When John G. was a very small boy, he was picked to play Joseph in the elementary school Christmas play. He had never stood up and talked or performed in front of people, especially adults before, and his parents had not encouraged open expression; to the contrary, he came from a rather old-fashioned home where children were expected to be "seen but not heard," and when other adults came to visit, the youngsters were instantly banished to the bedroom. As the evening premiere of the play grew closer, he grew more and more anxious. His imagination ran amok, negatively: what would happen if he mis-spoke his lines? Tripped and fell? On opening night, he was in a state of high anxiety. When he walked out onto the stage, he saw several hundred people in the audience. He knew his parents, grandparents and neighbors were there. He made eye contact with his mother and saw hope and anticipation in her eyes, as she waited for her son to make her proud. He made eye contact with a classmate not in the play, sitting in the front row with her parents; a little girl he thought was "cute." And he froze. He could not remember his lines. And, to his and everybody's mortification, he wet himself.

For days afterward, John refused to go to school, even to leave his bed, feigning sickness. No amount of consolation from his mother helped. And his father, quite embarrassed by his son's failure, avoided him—and John got that message loud and clear.

More than 35 years after this incident, John was able to describe it in vivid, precise detail, much more so than I have here. And planted in his mind was this sequence of connections: *fear* → *women* → *failure* → *humiliation*.

When he returned to school, as you'd imagine, his peers were vicious and unrelenting. He recalls the girls being the worst, groups of them pointing and laughing as he walked by.

In the passing years at school, John did everything he could to avoid standing up and speaking in class, and teachers, presumably sympathetic to his plight, avoided calling on him. He never dreamed of joining speech, drama, or debate class. The only school activity he joined was the chess club.

In junior high school, when he managed to muster the courage to ask a particular girl he'd had his eyes on all year to the first school dance, he was tongue-tied, stumbled over his words, and flushed red with embarrassment. To his horror, she didn't just turn him down; she laughed at him. "I'd be afraid all night that you'd pee on yourself," she said. And she said it loudly, so others could hear.

I could go on, because such experiences breed similar experiences, but you get the idea. All of this has made a very firm and deep imprint on John's self-image. In his mind's eye, he sees himself as a person unappealing to women, certain to be rejected by them, unable to conduct himself well in approaching them, and likely to be humiliated. "I'm just no good at meeting women" he says. His self-image accepts that conclusion wholeheartedly.

This is where the *Servo-Mechanism*—or "servant" mechanism— comes in. It is an awesomely powerful servant, and armed with all of your memory, knowledge and experience, with tremendous persuasive ability, physical energy, even powers we do not fully understand or appreciate, such as that commonly called extrasensory perception or ESP. Of greatest interest and importance is that this powerful servant has no bias whatsoever toward your success or failure, happiness or misery. It simply does as it is told by your self-image. If the self-image says "I'm no good at meeting women—keep me safe from such a terrible, terrifying situation," the Servo-Mechanism does exactly that.

John's Servo-Mechanism will cause him to turn down invitations to group events where he might meet women, will help him bury himself in work so he has no time for a social life, will give him unpleasant mannerisms or habits that turn women off and keep them away from him, and will make certain he is tongue-tied and ineffective if he does meet one, so that the encounter is brief.

Should John determine to force himself, with all the willpower he can muster, to go to a social event, introduce himself around, and engage women in conversation, he will fight enormous resistance manufactured by his very own self-image.

Now here is the big question: is John *really* "no good at" meeting women? Is this the *truth* about John?

Of course, it is not true. No one is born either good or bad at meeting and captivating members of the opposite sex. It is not genetic. Plus, there is plenty of empirical evidence to suggest that John could and should be "good at" meeting and conversing with women; he *is* good at conversing with men and women in nonsocial, nonintimate environments. He *is* bright, well-read, articulate, and witty. He has a warm and friendly personality. He is certainly physically capable of walking over to a woman, presenting friendly and nonthreatening body language, and engaging in pleasant conversation. No, it is not true that John is "no good at" this. But it *is* true his self-image makes him think this.

What does all this have to do with your sales call reluctance or procrastination? Everything, because John G. is living with his own kind of call reluctance.

My Favorite Call-Reluctance Story

I was told this story about a young married couple who got into a home-based direct sales business in their spare time. This required them to invite neighbors, friends, co-workers and other people they knew to evening meetings at their home, by calling them on the phone. They were embarrassed to make calls in front of each other, so each Monday evening, she would go into the bedroom, he would go into the downstairs den, and they took turns making calls. When she finished a call, she'd yell downstairs: "Your turn." Then when he finished, he'd yell upstairs "Your turn."

After three consecutive Thursday-evening meetings, it dawned on her that the only people showing up were the ones she invited. He had a 100% no-show rate. How could that be?

She decided to see for herself what he was saying to turn people off. She yelled "Your turn," then hurried downstairs and stuck her ear to the den door, where she heard him saying: "One thousand six, one thousand seven, one thousand eight, one thousand nine . . . honey, your turn!"

What makes grown, mature adults behave like juveniles when it comes to making sales calls? Look inside the self-image.

Why We Must Question What the Self-Image Believes

It is rather amazing to realize that you have, inside yourself, this thing we are calling the self-image that exerts almost total control over what you are able to do, and that this thing may be making decisions for you based on completely false beliefs. The self-image acting on false beliefs rather than true beliefs manufactures tremendous resistance. Resistance occurs when your body, mind, and very soul are in conflict. It occurs when what you want to do is deemed "impossible" for you by your own self-image, and occurs when you try to override your self-image rather than properly reprogram it. This is why you will benefit by closely examining your self-image's accumulated and current beliefs. My "Case of the Man with Stubby Fingers" that follows illustrates this point perfectly.

One day a fellow came in to see me, to ask if I, a plastic surgeon, could do anything about his short, fat, stubby fingers.

Now this was not as unusual as you might think, for people were always coming in with an endlessly amazing array of deformities to be fixed or improvements to be made to the face or body. I have talked with many people who wanted their big ears made smaller, their small penises made larger, fat sucked out of their cheeks, fat injected into their lips, and on and on. Second, most of these people saw what they were unhappy about in much magnified and distorted size and shape. When they looked in the mirror, they didn't see, for example, slightly oversize ears; they saw elephant-sized ears. Anyway, this fellow wiggled his fingers in front of me, which were not nearly so short and fat as he described, and asked if I could somehow surgically alter them for the better. Here is how our conversation went; see what you can detect from it:

MM: Why do you want your fingers operated on?

BILL: Can't you see? They are much too short and stubby.

MM: They look fine to me. What difference does it make if your fingers are different in size or shape from mine or anyone else's?

BILL: Because I am sick of being clumsy.

MM: What do you mean?

BILL: I drop things. My fork at the dinner table. If we go to a Chinese restaurant, I can never use the chopsticks.

MM: Me neither.

BILL: But these damned fingers. I can't do anything. Catch a ball. Hammer a nail straight. Put up a shelf or hang a picture around the house.

MM: And this bothers you?

BILL: Of course. My wife jokes about it with our friends— about how she keeps the tools under lock and key so I can't do any damage. Right now, she is putting a birdhouse up in our backyard and she has hired a neighborhood boy to assemble it rather than having me do it.

MM: How does this make you feel?

BILL: The man of the house is supposed to fix things!

MM: I see. Did your father fix things?

BILL: You bet. Poppa could fix anything. And he never let me help because I was always so clumsy I broke things.

MM: Did he tell you that you were clumsy?

BILL: Yes, but he didn't need to. It was obvious. My older brother was good at using his hands like my Poppa. But my hands were never any good. Just getting through a meal without spilling something was a feat. Poppa said my hands just weren't made to hold a tool.

MM: What was that you said about catching a ball?

BILL: Nobody wanted me on their baseball teams because I couldn't catch the ball.

MM: Do you know that different boys mature at different speeds?

BILL: I suppose so. Yes.

MM: How long has it been since you've tried fixing anything around the house?

BILL: Oh, I only tried once, right after we got married. I was 19. That was 20 years ago. I tried to put in storm windows and I broke one.

MM: When you first learned to drive a car, how were you as a driver?

BILL: Okay I guess. I didn't have any accidents. But I had some near misses. I had trouble with the stick shift.

MM: Do you drive differently today?

BILL: Sure. I mean, it's automatic, right? You just do it, you don't think about it.

MM: Yes. Bill, when you first were sexually intimate with a girl or a woman, how old were you?

BILL: 18.

MM: How was that?

BILL: (*Laughter.*) Okay for me but not much for her. I was pretty quick on the trigger, if you know what I mean.

MM: Has the way you make love changed since you were 18?

BILL: Of course.

MM: Isn't that a very physical act?

BILL: Yes. Partly. Oh, and I see what you're getting at. But you don't understand; my hands are a problem. Just my hands.

MM: Have you ever made anything? Painted anything? Put a toy together at Christmas? Anything like that?

BILL: I sometimes work jigsaw puzzles.

MM: You look at all the pieces, and visualize how they fit together to make the picture. You pick up those thin paperboard pieces with your fingers and fit them together. Right?

BILL: Yes.

MM: I want you to try a few things for the next 30 days before we get serious about operating on your hands. If you will try these suggestions earnestly and you still want me to operate on your fingers a month from now, I promise we will discuss the details then. All right?

BILL: Okay.

MM: These are my prescriptions and you must follow them to the letter, just as you would a prescription for dosage size and times to take pills prescribed to you. All right?

BILL: Yes.

MM: First, I want you to take a half an hour every day, and go to a quiet, private place. It could be the stall in the washroom during your lunch hour, or better, in your car, parked under a shade tree. Anywhere. Close your eyes. First, picture yourself working and quickly completing a very difficult jigsaw puzzle. Make your movie camera zoom in on your fingers picking up the puzzle pieces and fitting them in place. Be aware of how you see what the finished puzzle is to look like in your mind. Be aware of how it feels to pick up each piece and place it neatly where it belongs. How it *feels*.

Second, see yourself pushing the successfully completed puzzle aside and going to work on a more difficult task: putting together a model car kit purchased from the toy store. Visualize the little parts, the glue. You get the picture in your mind of how it is to look when finished, just like you do the puzzle. You pick up one piece at a time in your fingers and carefully fit it into place. See yourself doing all this flawlessly.

Third, you set the completed model aside, lay your hands flat on the table, fingers splayed out, and picture them growing longer and thinner, longer and thinner. See them playing the piano. See them closing tightly around a baseball after it plummets from the sky. Create this incredible mental movie and play it over and over again every day for 21 days in a row without fail. You may think that this is childish or silly, but I want you, no, I demand that you set aside those thoughts and honor this prescription to the very best of your ability.

Also, I want you to start a list. Take a piece of paper with lines on it, to write on. Draw a big line down the middle. On the left side, list everything you can think of you did badly or goofed up on as a child. Did you ever wet the bed? Write that down. Did you keep a horribly messy room? Write that down. Did you fail math? Write that down. Keep the list with you and add to it whenever you think of anything.

On the 22nd day, I want you to take a little time and fill in the right side of this page. If you now do the thing or something much like it well that you messed up as a kid, write down what you do well. Let's say you failed math but now you do complex price quotations every day. Write that down.

On the 22nd day, I want you to go to a hobby store and buy a car model, glue, and tools. Don't let anyone know you are working on it, but somewhere, secretly, spend that half hour a day building the model. If you make a mistake, although I don't think you will, say to yourself: I am a mistake maker but I am also a mistake breaker, I can do better, and this is only a toy anyway. Go buy another one and start over. When you get the model finished, come and show it to me.

One other thing. I want you to get a book from the library on how to tie all different kinds of knots. And buy some twine. Each day, tie one of the knots the way the book shows you. But take time to first picture both the finished knot and the process of tying it with your new slim, elongated piano player's fingers in your mind.

I did not see or hear from Bill for several months and I had frankly forgotten all about him. He dropped in unexpectedly one morning carrying a rather large box. Inside was a very complex, hand-built model of a sailing schooner, resemblant of the ship in the painting representing Psycho-Cybernetics that Salvador Dali painted and gave to me, that hangs in my office. The model ship had intricate details: little ropes, door handles, railings and such.

"I built this with my own hands as a gift for you," Bill said.

"Thank you," I said, "but what about our plans to operate on your clumsy fingers?"

Bill laughed. "Look, I got your message before the 20 days were over with. I realized my fingers weren't at fault, that it was what I believed about them that caused me to be clumsy. I *thought* clumsy, so I *was* clumsy. And maybe I was clumsy when I was a kid but I was a lot of other things when I was a kid that I'm not now. Heck, I actually think my fingers got a bit thinner. Anyway, I won't be needing that surgery."

"Darn good thing," I said, "because there is no such thing as a surgical operation to lengthen and slim fingers."

As you can see, Bill was letting his past control his present and determine his future—unquestioned, unchallenged. But what was true about Bill—or for that matter you—20 years, 2 years or 20 months ago may not be true today. And it certainly does *not* have to remain true! That is up to you.

> # "I am a Mistake Maker, but I am also a Mistake Breaker."

How We Specifically Apply This to Conquering Call Reluctance

As it is with most things, a problem honestly acknowledged is at least half solved. If you will confront your habit of avoidance and take it on with the determination to chase it out of your daily life, this alone is much more than just the first step of a lengthy journey; instead, it is a giant leap toward success. A leap that puts you perhaps halfway to your goal.

Over the years, I have met and had lengthy conversations with many top sales professionals. Almost without exception, these men and women had struggled at some point in their careers and ultimately made a decision, a commitment to move from avoidance to confrontation. I don't mean confrontation in the negative sense, by the way. I mean confronting your own demons with determination. Having the commitment to rid yourself and your life of any particular demon, in this case, call reluctance, is almost magical in its power.

Once you are committed to this course of action, genuinely determined to surgically remove call reluctance or call avoidance from your life, then I can suggest five practical steps certain to yield fast, positive results.

Step One: Choose Prospects You Can Feel Good About Calling or Calling on

Frankly, this is outside my area of expertise, so I'll only indulge in a very brief discussion. It does seem to me that call reluctance is most likely to increase and intensify in proportion to how little you know about the prospects and how little belief you have in their interest in what you have to offer. Consider *Glengarry Glen Ross*, starring Al Pacino, a movie about real estate salespeople based on David Mamet's brilliant play. In it, the salespeople were walking, talking, living call reluctance. They had no confidence whatsoever in the value of the leads they had to call. It is probable, then, that call reluctance diminishes in proportion to how much you know about your prospects and how much interest you think they have in what you have to offer.

When I was booking myself to lecture on the subject of Psycho-Cybernetics, if someone called into the office and gave my wife a message like "We want to book Dr. Maltz to speak at the Met Life Convention in August. Please let us know if he has August 8th open and how much to make the check out for," I was very eager to return that call. Let me at the phone! But if a Met Life agent gave me the name of a regional sales manager who was on the committee to choose speakers for the next convention and suggested I call and introduce myself to him, I was not all that eager to make the call.

You see, I am a human being just like you, with ordinary human emotions and frailties. You and I are very much alike. We may be able to force ourselves, with mature will and self-discipline, to do certain unpleasant things in order to get very desirable results. But it is almost impossible to force ourselves to do so consistently.

Willpower disappoints. Instead, it makes sense to engineer a combination of pleasant activity leading to desired results whenever possible, doesn't it?

The smartest sales professionals I know creatively find ways to put themselves in the first kind of situation a lot: where they are calling only prospects who have expressed great interest and are very likely to buy. It's "a leg up" to create situations where your anticipation is positive, where your expectation of the call is that it will be a pleasant experience.

However, don't fall into the trap of blaming the quality of your prospects. This can be very unproductive. There is something you can do to secure better prospects *and* improve the quality of the ones you have to work with.

For example, take our young couple, she making calls, he hiding in the den only pretending to make calls. One of the things that eventually helped him was carefully going through his prospect list and identifying something he knew about each person that could give that person reason for interest in the business proposition. One guy loved fishing, so "what if you could easily make enough extra money to pay for a vacation cabin on a lake and go fishing a lot more?" Another had two kids in junior high, so "how will you pay for their college education?" And so on. This thinking process raised the value of the prospects in his mind, so he had more optimism and enthusiasm for calling and talking with them.

In terms of selling technique, working out sophisticated ways to attract and obtain highly qualified prospects can not only wipe out call avoidance, but also automatically improve your success at closing sales. Most sales professionals have been indoctrinated in "if you tell your story to enough people, some will buy." The virtues of hard work and persistence are held up as the answer to just about every selling problem, from call avoidance to poor closing ratios. But three of my co-authors (Brooks, Kennedy, Yellen) will tell you that this is as antiquated as using a washboard or farming with horse-drawn plows. These days, the most successful sales professionals learn very sophisticated strategies of prescreening and presorting prospects before meeting with them in person or getting on the telephone with them.

Step Two: Being 110% Sold on What You Are Selling

Have you heard the phrase "have the courage of your convictions?" Tough to have "courage" if you have no "convictions." The most convincing salespeople are the most convinced of the merits of their own proposition. I was such a powerful advocate for the profession of plastic surgery because of the strength of my convictions. And I believe the almost unrivaled success of Psycho-Cybernetics has emanated from the power of my own convictions. While this seems obvious, would it surprise you to hear that the majority of the salespeople I have met and counseled over the years have *not* been totally, passionately, unwaveringly convinced of the superior value and worth of what they represented?

Even worse, I occasionally discovered salespeople who were not at all convinced that their prospects had to have and would benefit enormously from what they offered. In truth, they felt like they were often pressing people to buy something they did not need or wasn't the best, pressing them to spend money they might put to better use. What imprint would such a feeling make on the self-image? *Con artist. Someone undeserving of success and prosperity, deserving of guilt and unhappiness.* Such a self-image would command the Servo-Mechanism to deliver just that: an abundance of misery and unhappiness.

You must go inside your own mind and use your product and business knowledge, knowledge of your prospects' needs and desires, and your creative imagination to build up a strong sense of pride for what you offer. You must develop an understanding of the profound superiority, worth, and importance of your product, so that you can't wait for the next opportunity to tell someone about it. And if you are trying to sell something you cannot feel that way about, my frank advice would be to find something more meritorious to sell.

Selling is all about *trust.* How can you expect others to trust you if you feel untrustworthy? Surely the sales professional lacking belief in the superiority of what he or she has to offer and the "match" of the offer with a prospect must have a sick feeling in the pit of his/her stomach when sitting down at a desk facing the telephone.

You must also go inside your own mind and use your knowledge and experience of the good your product does, of the quality of the advice you give your clients, of your own integrity, communication ability, persuasive talents, and personal enthusiasm to build up your self-image as a sales professional. How *do* you see yourself as a sales professional? Beggar or highly skilled, appreciated and respected expert? "Taker" or customer-oriented problem solver? At the bottom of the business totem pole, or as one of the most important people in the corporation as well as the driving force of the American economy? As at least an equal of the prospects you are calling on and clients you are serving?

I would propose that a great deal of call reluctance is a representation of the sales professional's poor self-image! Strengthen the self-image and watch both your call reluctance and others' resistance to your prospecting efforts melt away!

Step Three: Recalling Past Accomplishments

This is a simple Psycho-Cybernetic Technique now commonplace among the most successful amateur and pro athletes, salespeople, speakers, writers, and people of all walks of life trying to get "over the hump" of fear, doubt, and reluctance, into productive action.

If you have been in the habit of living fearfully or skeptically, your self-image has recollections of frustrations, disappointments, and failures conveniently within reach, which pop up at the slightest provocation. This turns the Servo-Mechanism into a failure-seeking missile, dragging you toward such a target.

Consider the salesperson who has exercised little control over self-image, and is on her way to front a booth for her company at a trade show. She says to herself:

"Another trade show. What a waste of time. Everybody's just a looky-loo. I never write any business at these shows. The leads I get don't pan out. I worked for three days at that show a month ago and still haven't got a single contract to show for it."

As an aside, I'd note that this woman is blaming everything but herself, and would be well served by asking herself tough questions about the attitude, preparation, knowledge, game plan and energy she carried into that last trade show.

But what she must do now is determine that history is *not* going to repeat itself. That she is clever and creative enough to out-smart what she has experienced as a difficult selling environment. That while others complain about being stuck there and spend their days eating doughnuts and handing out brochures and their nights playing poker and sympathizing with each other, she will use the time there productively to identify key prospects for assertive fol-low-up, meeting with clients and prospects over dinner, and, evenings, calling and inviting prospects to visit her at her booth.

She can help and encourage herself by recalling and feeding the self-image any and all evidence obtainable to support such ideas. For example: "There was this time when I was placed in another situation you'd think nobody could sell in, but I figured out how to do it, with a clever idea. If I did it there, I can do it here."

For example:"I am the kind of person who outperforms my col-leagues all the time. The proof is that most recent contest when . . ." Or: "Remember that show I worked my first year? I didn't know any better, had all kinds of enthusiasm, and actually wrote several big orders with new customers right on the spot. Maybe I need to rekin-dle some of that energy . . ."

With this kind of thinking, you can turn your Servo-Mechanism into a success-seeking guided missile that will pull you toward that target!

Step Four: Mental Rehearsal

There's just no substitute for success breeding success. But if you don't have much real experience making calls, how can you build success on top of success? The answer is *synthetic experience.* One of the greatest gifts contained inside the human imagina-tion—and one of the greatest liabilities contained in the human imagination—is the fact that your entire system, mind and body, can be just as affected by synthetic experience as by real experience.

You know that you can make yourself physically sick by think-ing sick. Kids elevate their temperatures and get sick to their stom-achs in order to skip school by imagining themselves sick. Once a man came to me and confessed that he had ruined his marriage and driven away his wife by imagining that she was cheating on him. Even though he had no physical proof, no logical reason to even suspect this was happening, she was very beautiful, younger than he, and he had begun imagining her having sex with this person or that person they both knew. The images grew more and more vivid and produced real jealousy and resentment. Soon he was impotent in the bedroom and irritable and hot-tempered everywhere else, dominated by his negative imagination. He began to mentally play out what he would do to any man he caught her cheating with. His only satisfaction came from these mental movies of finally catching his wife's secret lover and beating him within an inch of his life.

One day he arrived home from work early, encountered a man walking out of the master bedroom, and assaulted him, breaking his nose and his arm, and sending him to the hospital. Unfortunately, the man was a carpet cleaner there that day cleaning the carpets. For his wife, it was the last straw. For him, synthetic experience was just as real and action-causing as real experience. Of course, this is a very negative and unhappy example. But it can work for good with just as much impact.

So, if you will develop the perfect telephone prospecting call or walk-in call as a very vivid mental movie, with the positive outcomes exactly as you desire them, you can begin daily *Mental Rehearsal*, quickly enhancing your desire to make calls and dissolving your call reluctance.

Mental Rehearsal is used by top athletes of every type, top business negotiators and trial lawyers, actors and entertainers, even surgeons like myself. When I get the opportunity to quiz a leading sales professional in any given organization about this, I find many practitioners of Mental Rehearsal.

One of America's most famous and successful trial lawyers, Gerry Spence, author of the book *How to Argue and Win Every Time* talks about mentally visualizing himself delivering his summation. Using his imagination, he hears the tonality of his voice, and sees the jurors responding, comprehending, nodding in agreement. By the time he actually delivers this speech, it is simply deja vu.

In this way, the pro who uses daily Mental Rehearsal conquers avoidance, enhances confidence, and establishes a pattern of success that builds on itself.

Step Five: Relaxation

If you feel a little ball of tension appear in your stomach when you sit down at your desk to make telephone calls, you will be better served by taking a few minutes to relax than by forcing yourself to pick up the phone. Think of it as persuading yourself vs. arguing with yourself. *Persuasion* diffuses and diminishes resistance; *argument* usually increases and strengthens resistance.

Don't take these few minutes to escape, though. Don't pull your hand back from the telephone as if it were electrified, leave your chair, and escape into the bull session over at the coffee machine. Stay put, but go inside your own mind and replace resistance with relaxation.

There is a Psycho-Cybernetic Technique called *Calm Body, Calm Mind* many sales pros find very useful, right before beginning a series of telephone calls or walking in to make a presentation. Its premise is that it is easier to relax the body than to relax the mind, but that when you do relax the body, you automatically relax the mind. You might look at your behavior as a circle, and you can start anywhere in the circle. For example, thoughts cause feelings which cause actions, but actions also cause thoughts which cause feelings.

Five Steps to Conquering Call Reluctance

1. Choose prospects you can feel good about calling on

2. Be 110% sold on what you are selling

3. Recall past accomplishments

4. Use Mental Rehearsal

5. Relax!

Let's remember that there is no "purple heart award" in selling. You do not make a bigger commission by deliberately doing something the hard way rather than the easy way. If it is easier to relax the mind by first relaxing the body, why not use that strategy rather than trying to fight, to try and struggle against your natural impulses with teeth-gritted willpower?

Using *Calm Body, Calm Mind*, we start with physical actions in order to get to a calm, relaxed feeling. Here's the process:

> Find a comfortable place in which to sit or even lie down, in private. Close your eyes, go into the Theater of the Mind and enjoy a brief minimovie that is very relaxing to you. It might be a nature movie, or a walk through quiet, sunlit woods. Concentrate on the experience of the movie: the sights, sounds, smells. When the movie ends, use your imagination to put each part of your body in turn up on the screen: the back of your neck, each shoulder, arm, hand, etc., and each time see a heated cloth applied, the red and orange warmth penetrating the skin and softening the muscles. Visualize the muscles getting soft, even mushy. When you are done, say to yourself "Calm Body, Calm Mind" ten times, slowly. Take a deep breath in before saying it, let out the breath after saying it. Finally open your eyes, stand up and shake yourself, almost like a wet dog does. See how much looser you are?

Learning, practicing and mastering a relaxation regimen like this is very important. Having tension inside guarantees resistance on the outside. Conversely, relaxation inside will reduce resistance outside.

Dehypnosis and Call Reluctance

If you chronically, consistently procrastinate when it comes to making certain kinds of calls, what if I told you that you had been *hypnotized* to experience anxiety and discomfort when facing such calls?

No, I don't mean that some stage hypnotist in a black and red cape put you in a chair, waved a crystal in front of your face, put you "under," and imbedded paralyzing fears in your psyche. But everybody is hypnotized in different ways. Belief without current reason in anything is a result of some form of hypnosis. With a combination of other peoples' programming, your repetition of that same programming, along with some past experiences, your self-image can have been hypnotized to believe that certain types of calls are always painful, unpleasant, frustrating and unproductive.

I recall one automobile salesman telling me that he never called the leads distributed by the sales manager, that came from the company's national advertising, offering free literature by means of a toll-free number. When I asked why he didn't call these prospects, he said that they were old by the time he got them, didn't remember even asking for the information, had already bought cars and were resistant to being called by a car salesman. It took me two hours of counseling to dissect all that, but I'll summarize my findings for you. Why did he feel this way? What was his strong belief based on? Mostly because that's what all the other grizzled veteran salespeople at the dealership had told him. He had only called a few of these prospects, then stopped trying and, instead, joined in the "gripe sessions" at the soda machine about the lousy leads, dumb sales manager, and so on. The few calls he had made, he made expecting resistance—and got exactly what he expected.

This fellow was hypnotized, even paralyzed, when it came to calling prospects provided to him from advertising. It's possible, of course, that he was right about the value of these particular leads. But it's also possible he was wrong. He would never know, because he would never give the possibilities a fair test. Worse, this hypnosis will likely follow him throughout his entire selling career, preventing him from valuing and assertively following up on any leads furnished by any sales managers or derived from any advertising.

Are you hypnotized in one way or another? Dehypnotize yourself! Separate fact from opinion, experience from theory, the past from the present from the future. Dehypnotize yourself with relaxation, and with Mental Rehearsal. Take control of every aspect of your selling career!

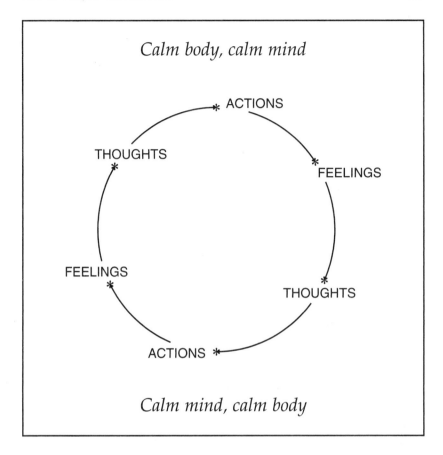

Quick Tips for Self-Dehypnosis

1. Identify a personal behavior that is holding you back or may be counterproductive.

2. Identify the attitudes, thoughts, and beliefs that support and produce that behavior. What is it that you believe, that causes you to do or avoid doing this particular thing?

3. Identify the input that has produced the belief. What were you taught? What have you heard from others? What have you experienced? What has manufactured and solidified this belief?

4. Now, analytically and carefully question each one of those sources for the belief. Are they validated by evidence or are they just opinions? Are they antiquated? Have conditions changed significantly since the idea was provided to you? Have you changed? Hold each individual, isolated "item" that has contributed to your governing belief up to the bright light of intelligent, unemotional scrutiny.

I suggest that you go through this process with pen and paper, not just in your mind.

Many times, I've guided someone through this process and watched them emerge from a hypnotized state, amazed at the lack of substance in what has been governing their behavior. But you do not need me to be your guide. You can dehypnotize yourself with your own mind, your own intelligence.

The Remarkable Secret of Emotional Antioxidants

Top sales professionals achieve and sustain peak mental, emotional and physical well-being. When you have successfully dehypnotized yourself from imbedded, erroneous, limiting beliefs, and you "feel good," resistance to you melts away, and you get good results.

Can it be this simple? That "feeling good" is the golden key to top success in selling? Yes, it can. That is why the subject of *emotional antioxidants* is so important.

You are undoubtedly aware of the many discoveries about certain antioxidants found in foods, notably leafy vegetables, that have a positive impact on the immune system by dramatically reducing risks of cancers as well as other diseases. For this reason, antioxidant vitamins are the most popular and universally respected nutritional supplements. Well, imagine being able to manufacture antioxidants inside your own mind, then pump them through your bloodstream, throughout your entire body!

As a man of medical science, I know that the key to physical well-being is a healthy immune system. As a student of the human mind, I uncovered the secret of the self-image, of which emotional well-being is the key. Now it is becoming increasingly apparent that there is a profound link between the two. Martin E.P. Seligman, a psychology professor at the University of Pennsylvania says: "There is evidence that optimism bolsters the immune system."

Unfortunately, optimism is massively misunderstood. Most people believe incorrectly that being optimistic means always feeling cheerful, happy and "positive," never acknowledging adversity, problems, or setbacks. This sets up an impossible standard. No human can "think positive" all the time. Certainly, no human can go through life having only positive experiences. No salesperson can go through life without experiencing call reluctance, procrastination, slumps, frustration and disappointment. Setbacks happen. Dr. Seligman describes optimism as a habitual way of constructively explaining setbacks to yourself.

If Dr. Seligman is correct, developing the habit of optimistic response may not only enhance your emotional well-being, it may also enhance your physical health. And I would point out that what Dr. Seligman has termed "the habit of optimistic response" is, in fact, Psycho-Cybernetics.

Imagine: you are going to now possess a simple style or method of thinking and continually programming your self-image that yields comprehensive benefits. This single method of thinking will heighten your immunity to negative and detrimental influences of all kinds, both physical and mental.

How to Use the Habit of Optimistic Response to Your Advantage

Many people drift into the habit of blaming undesirable experiences or outcomes on permanent conditions. For example, someone who delivers a speech badly, stumbles over words, and is not well received then says to his or her self-image: "I'm just not good at speaking in front of groups." This turns the unpleasant incident into a permanent condition. The self-image will subsequently turn this into an instruction given to the Servo-Mechanism every time this person steps to a podium to deliver a talk.

A genuine optimist acknowledges the existence of a permanent disadvantage only very reluctantly, in the face of overwhelming evidence, so, in the same situation, he or she would be more likely to say to the self-image: "I did not succeed with my speech, but I can learn to do better the next time."Then would go ahead and evaluate how he or she was introduced, organized material, spoke, used humor, dress, and so on, in search of ways to be better and do better. This is the habit of optimistic response in action.

How Simple Optimism Can Help You Open the Mind of a Difficult Prospect

Once a young salesman cornered me after a seminar, to complain passionately about the executive he had to deal with at one of his key accounts. "Every time I go to him with a new product, a new idea, a better way of doing things," George H. said, "he instantly shoots it down or brushes me off. How am I ever going to expand this account's value if I can't even get my ideas listened to? There's just no point in even telling this guy about anything new."

I asked, "How do you usually approach this fellow with your ideas?" I listened as the salesman described when and how he went to this customer with new products or ideas. He described what he said and what the client said.

"Does it always happen like that?"I inquired.

"Absolutely," the salesman said. "It's as if there was a script and we each read our parts."

"It might as well be," I told him. "As long as you make the same first move, he is going to make the same second move. You and he are having the same chess match over and over again. Because you are frustrated with this client, you keep approaching him exactly the same way, just waiting for his unsatisfactory response. And you get it. Let me tell you what a person with the habit of optimistic response might do. First, he would stop doing the same thing over and over. Second, he would know two things in his heart: one, that this person can be reached, interested, opened up, even inspired—because every human being can be! Third, he would keep trying different approaches until one proved effective."

I suppose this seems like common sense when you read it on the printed page, but believe me, it is quite uncommon in real life.

The world is full of people who continue doing the same thing over and over again even though it produces unsatisfactory results each and every time. A great deal of call reluctance develops by doing the same unproductive thing, using the same unproductive approach over and over again, eventually producing the erroneous but governing belief in the existence of a permanent condition—either "cold calling doesn't work in this business" or "I can't cold call" or something along those lines.

How to Cultivate the Habit of Optimistic Response

1. When you feel frustrated—STOP! Ask yourself if you are giving the power of permanence to something that can be changed. Are you struggling with an unpleasant incident, a temporary set of circumstances, or a permanent condition? Rarely will you be able to support the notion of a permanent condition.

2. Tell your self-image: "I can figure this out."

3. Remind your self-image of your past achievements that indicate you can figure this out, that you can do better in this situation.

4. Be alert for patternistic behavior, doing the same thing the same way, when doing so has been producing unsatisfactory results. Break the pattern!

Optimistic responses dismantle resistance!

A Special Warning to Sales Managers

Sales managers are often frustrated by the sales professionals on their teams who exhibit significant talent and potential, but seem to avoid making the necessary calls to do well, to put themselves in a position to succeed. It mystifies the manager to watch the salesperson repeatedly turn his or her back on opportunity. The manager will cajole, threaten, and nag this salesperson about following up on the leads and making those calls, but this never works. Gradually, frustration escalates, the relationship is destroyed by this cancer, the manager fires the salesperson or the salesperson quits.

In some businesses, like life insurance, for example, or network marketing, for another, this loss of promising sales professionals—usually called "turnover"—occurs at an incredible rate. In some sales organizations, dozens and dozens of salespeople come and quickly go before one stays and goes on to some measure of success. In the insurance industry, many companies or General Agents incur expenses totalling as much as $10,000 to recruit, hire, and train one new agent, only to lose within the first year. Such "turnover" is the plague of sales organizations.

If you have turnover in your organization like this, you must turn over a new leaf today; you must refuse to accept it as the norm. It may be the norm in your industry but that does not mean it must be the norm in your organization. You aren't in control of your industry but, my friend, you are in control of your organization. You can change its culture, its environment, your expectations, and the expectations of the people you employ.

Many sales managers simply chalk all this failure up to these people being "losers." Weak spirited, weak minded, lazy. But I would caution the Sales Manager about taking such an easy out. Some of the quitters may be better served to find other work, in a different occupation. But in most cases, the person came to your organization sincerely, even enthusiastically looking for the opportunity to succeed. No one comes to selling thinking it will be easy or planning on being lazy. They know they must work. These are *not* losers. If they lose, if they fail, it is partially their own fault but quite probably, partially yours too. After all, what is your job? Isn't it to find the right way to draw the best out of each different individual?

You must be very, very cautious about branding anybody a "loser." Think of the pro sports coaches who have been embarrassed by cutting players they viewed as underachievers only to have those players become superstars on another team, for a competing coach. An individual may be *blocked* from achievement by many different things, but he or she is not simply a "loser" or "underachiever."

Like a good doctor, like me when interviewing and counseling a patient, the astute sales manager learns to differentiate between symptoms and causes, between labels and truths.

There really is no such disease as call reluctance. The sharp sales manager understands this, so when he or she has someone in the organization exhibiting this behavior, he/she takes the time and invests the effort to dig deep and counsel that person, to work on the real problem. Pointing your finger and saying the person suffers from call reluctance won't help. Shaking your fist or pounding your shoe on the desk and demanding the person makes those calls will not prove productive. Threats fail. Nagging fails.

I take enormous care to avoid branding anyone a "loser," "lazy," or with any other negative label, and I urge sales managers, teachers and coaches to resist this easy temptation too. Every individual has seeds of greatness within, and desire to succeed, but every individual also comes to an organization with some baggage. A great sales manager sees the greatness in the individual and sets about to systematically, strategically, and compassionately unleash that potential.

With all that in mind, on the following page appears an essay I wrote in 1959, that managers and coaches may find value in posting in their offices, as a reminder of what developing people is all about.

LOOK INSIDE THE HUSK
by Dr. Maxwell Maltz

*And what is a weed? A plant whose virtues
have not been discovered.*

—RALPH WALDO EMERSON

WHEN DID THESE splendid words occur to Emerson? Perhaps one day when the harvest was ready to be gathered home and the bright fields rippled in the wind, wheat for the winter's bread. For, ages ago, wheat was thought to be a weed, quite useless to mankind.

Perhaps on that day, looking at the ripe bronze fields, Emerson was returning from a visit to his friend the teacher Bronson Alcott—that tireless, undefeatable, unquenchable man—and paused to reflect on Alcott's stubborn insistence that it was never the "bad boy" or the dullard who was to blame but those who lacked the patience and the care to probe beneath the surface for what was good, however unpromising or unfriendly that surface might be. There were no "weeds" in Bronson Alcott's schoolroom.

So many times, in clinic and hospital ward, have I seen the apparently hopeless misfit transformed into a hopeful and helpful person—a giver, not a taker—by the simplest display of interest and belief in him. It always makes me wonder how many good citizens, creators and builders and contributors to our common health as a nation, have been lost because someone, somewhere, was misled by the husk and did not see the golden grain within.

I suppose it comes down to this: Our first "must" for every day should be to pause before passing judgment, remembering that the apparently useless weed in the dirt of the roadside may, with care and cultivation, provide tomorrow's bread.

Chapter 2

How to Anticipate and Easily Eliminate Stalls and Objections

You've worked hard to secure the appointment with your prospect. You prepared. Maybe you listened to a "pep talk" tape in the car, on the way to the appointment. You delivered a virtuoso presentation. But just as you get ready to pop the closing question and get his John Hancock on the dotted line, he whips out an objection. Now the ping-pong begins. He tosses out an objection; you answer. He comes up with a stall; you overcome it. Back and forth. Back and forth.

The first thing you should know about stalls and objections is that, in most cases, they shouldn't occur at all. If you do encounter them frequently, it signals fundamental weaknesses in one of three areas: prospecting, positioning, or presenting. Let's set that aside for the moment, though, and talk about the actual handling of objections when they do occur.

A Man Bedeviled by Objections

I was speaking for a large insurance company at their national sales conference, and had agreed to have breakfast with one of their agents, Richard, who had contacted me ahead of time and asked for a few private minutes. Here's our conversation; see if you can diagnose his problem.

RICHARD: Dr. Maltz, thank you for taking your time with me. I've read your books and they've helped me tremendously.

MM: I'm glad.

RICHARD: There's just one problem . . .

MM: Yes?

RICHARD: My sales are down because of all the objections I keep getting. I do okay at securing appointments and getting in front of people. But when I'm winding up my presentation, I can ask for the order, the prospects start coming up with one troublesome objection after another.

MM: Do all your prospects do this?

RICHARD: Yes! It's as if they all had the same script.

MM: And they keep raising the same objections?

RICHARD: Yes. Would you like to know what their objections are?

MM: Good heavens no! It's bad enough you must listen to them. I certainly don't want to. What I would like to hear is what you are doing about them.

RICHARD: Well, I answer them as best I can.

MM: Do you get through them to make sales?

RICHARD: Not very often.

MM: Do you answer them pretty much the same way every time you run up against them?

RICHARD: Yes. Sure. I told you, I give them my best answers.

MM: But these answers don't work.

RICHARD: No. I guess not.

MM: So what are you doing to resolve this?

RICHARD: Nothing. I mean, what can I do but give my best answers?

Well, what's your diagnosis? I can tell you this: you can't solve a problem by *not* working on it. Doing the same thing repeatedly but hoping for vastly different results is foolish. You cannot plant radish seeds and hope for tomatoes. You cannot keep running in the same futile circle and achieve different results just by running harder or faster; you must do something to break out of that vicious circle!

There's an old medical joke: the patient says, "Doctor, it hurts like hell when I do this," and the doctor says, "Don't do that." This was the first part of my prescription for this fellow; stop giving back those same answers. They're not working for you, so put them away and forget about them. You need new, different and better responses that you can have confidence in. I suggested the following as well:

1. Corral the two or three most successful agents you know here at this conference and trade them the best steak dinner in town for picking their brain, to learn how they respond to these objections. Get your ego out of your way and seek information from these top performers.

By the way, what an enemy of progress the human ego can be! The ego drives us to keep doing the same unproductive things, and unreasonably keeps us hoping for different, productive results. The ego prevents us men from doing something as simple and sensible as admitting that we are lost and stopping at a service station to ask a local resident for directions. The ego very often gets in the way of one professional going to his or her peers and colleagues for advice. But ego can never solve your problems, lead you to a breakthrough in understanding, guide you to a better idea, or pay your bills! If you are temporarily struggling with something like clients' objections derailing your sales, you must not let your own ego stand in the way of seeking ideas and advice.

2. Pick a prospect or two or three out of last month's group that didn't do business with you, go back, make it clear you are not trying to sell them a thing, only to learn, and talk with them about the objections they raised, why they raised them, why they were not responsive. Try to learn something.

A woman entrepreneur, the owner of a small computer consulting company told me she was having no trouble locating, con-
tacting and securing appointments with qualified prospects, but that
most of them cut her time with them short and rather brusquely
hurried her out of their offices. She thought it might be a gender
problem: successful male executives not taking an attractive, young
woman seriously in business. As I listened to her describe these very
unsuccessful sales presentations, I was convinced it was more than
that. I suggested she go back to a few of these businessmen and very
sincerely, openly ask for their critique of her presentation, for their
help in better presenting her company's capabilities.

A year later, I again visited with this woman, and she had a
great deal of success to report. In fact, her business had grown so
quickly, she now had three account representatives working for her,
and she no longer made sales calls herself. Her willingness to set
aside her ego, open herself up to criticism, even to risk and endure
some embarrassment led to discovery of exactly the insights she
needed to connect with her prospective clients.

When she had returned a few weeks later, she told me that
one of the three executives she approached on this basis spent
nearly three hours with her in his office, explaining in precise
detail what she had said that had closed his mind, what doubts
and concerns he had about using her type of company's services
she had not addressed, and why he had quickly decided not to
take her seriously. He brought in his own top salesperson to give
her some additional ideas. And he invited her back in a month to
make a new presentation. She said that listening to him cut her
apart was painful, but she knew that what he was telling her had
merit and was not said maliciously, so she forced herself to set
aside her ego, fought her impulse to be defensive, listened carefully, and then spent a couple of days carefully, unemotionally evaluating everything she had been told. Do you have the courage to
"ask for directions"?

3. Get some fresh training. I pointed out to him that there
was a workshop right there at the conference—"How to Sell When
the Client Says No"—that he had planned on attending. Did he
attend? No, he admitted. Why on earth not, I thought to myself.

4. Enlist the assistance of the Servo-Mechanism. I told him to, each day, take at least 30 to 60 minutes of quiet, private time, to go into the Theater of Your Mind. To take a comfortable seat, and call up mental movies of his most successful sales, of the first time he sold to the individuals who are now his best clients. If they raised objections, watch the movie carefully to see how he handled them then. I told him to give his Servo-Mechanism some fresh experience with his successes, to invigorate it as a Success Mechanism.

Right now, this fellow's Servo-Mechanism is functioning very effectively as an Automatic Failure Mechanism. His self-image told it he was the guy who got the worst leads, who prepared to do his best but was disappointed over and over again, whose best answers weren't good enough, and who had to struggle mightily to make a sale. His Servo-Mechanism made sure his experiences lived up to that set of directives. It quietly, sometimes imperceptibly, guided him to that result just as the technology installed in guided missiles gets them to the preprogrammed targets. He had to break free of that vicious circle. I explained all that to him, and urged him to use the Theater of Your Mind to run very different movies of success and accomplishment, to feed the Servo-Mechanism a different diet for a while.

5. Finally I told him: as you develop new ways of responding to these objections, use them in mental rehearsal. Give the perfect presentation and easily overcome the objections inside your own mind. Replay that several times each day.

I explained to Richard that there is rarely a straight line from point A to point B in our lives. That's why the Servo-Mechanism is designed to respond to feedback, correct its course, and zig-zag its way to the goals it is programmed to achieve.

The objections Richard was encountering repeatedly were negative feedback. Given the right information, his Servo-Mechanism would correct its course and provide him with better responses to the objections. He was blocking this natural process with pessimistic feelings, a "poor me" attitude, and foolish repetition of the same ineffective behavior. To unblock, I told Richard he had to view these experiences as a message trying to get through to

The Theater of Your Mind

The Theater of Your Mind is constructed in your imagination much like a real theater, with a huge screen and comfortable, plush chairs.

It is your private theater, so you can ask that any movie be shown. When you sit down to watch a movie, be sure you create that movie in vivid detail, to reinforce encouraging, self-image-strengthening messages.

Anytime you like, you can stop the movie, get up from your comfortable seat, and step into the scene. Take note of the sounds, the colors, the feelings you experience being there. Return to your seat and let the movie continue. Once you have carefully created a particular movie, you can store it in the projector room, and ask to have it shown again any time you return to the Theater.

These times that you choose to view the same mental movie repeatedly will not require the deliberate thought the first viewing did, when you were making the movie and viewing it at the same time, so you will be able to sit back, relax and enjoy the experience of the movie.

him about how he could be much more successful in selling, he had to warmly receive the message, use it as inspiration to actively seek out better solutions than he already possessed, and as stimulus to change. With that, I sent Richard on his way.

A few months later, I got this letter from Richard:

Dear Dr. Maltz,

It may surprise you to know that the sad-sack salesman you talked with in the coffee shop at the insurance convention less than six months ago is now the number-two man in this entire region! It still surprises me a bit!

I thought you would like to know that I followed your advice to the letter. As I look back on these few weeks, I can best explain it by saying that I constructed a whole new Richard inside my mind, and as I got that right, what went on in my actual sales interviews changed dramatically. Prospects seemed to pay closer attention to the points I made, had more trust in me, and now accept my recommendations without hesitation.

What Richard experienced was the powerful connection between the self-image, how you really see yourself, and how others see you.

Four Ways to Mentally and Emotionally Respond to Stalls and Objections

Your first—and worst—option is to respond with anger, frustration and resentment. Or the second option is to respond as Richard did, with stubborn, dumb persistence. Third, you could respond by being a victim and blame the clients or circumstances beyond your control. Or, finally fourth, my choice: you can be inspired and motivated to seek new opportunities, to correct your course, and to rise above the frustration. *You* make this choice. *No one* makes it for you.

If you respond with anger, frustration and resentment, you turn off your Success Mechanism and turn on your Failure Mechanism. These three are very destructive, dangerous emotions.

They are, in my opinion, actually cancerous. It will not surprise me if medical science eventually discovers that immersion in these emotions is a cause of cancer just as surely as is smoking large quantities of tobacco or living in the shadow of a factory dispelling toxic fumes.

But more immediately, anger clouds the mind, so that accurate, analytical thought is impossible. Imagine being put inside one of those giant mazes that are in some royal gardens in Europe. You must use your wits to find your way out. You must remain calm, try this path; if you meet a dead-end, you must reverse, correct, and move in another direction. It may take you hours of patient movement to find the exit. Or you may do it in minutes. But if you lose your temper and get angry at the maze, and give yourself up to anger, it can only take longer to escape. Time can only be lost to standing there in the maze screaming at it or ripping and flailing at its walls with your hands. It could care less. It will not budge. You can only escape by looking for the exit, not by being angry.

When you walk out of a meeting where a prospect's stalls and objections have blocked your achievement, if you realize you are angry at those objections or angry at the prospect or angry at anybody or anything, stop—don't rush headlong toward the next disaster. Don't even risk your life by getting behind the steering wheel of your car with steam coming out of your ears. Go and find a quiet park bench on which to sit, get a small mirror out of your jacket pocket or handbag, look yourself in the eye and ask yourself what good your anger is doing you. Ask how your anger can help. Tell yourself: "my friend, baying at the moon like some bewildered animal is not me. I am smarter than that. More mature than that." Go ahead and laugh at yourself. Think about what a funny thing it is for a grown adult to give up all of his intelligence and authority to anger, like a child banging a displeasing toy on the ground. In your mind, call up a picture of yourself as a child, furiously banging some toy on the ground until you break it, having made the situation worse, not better, with your childish anger. See yourself crying and wailing in frustration and unhappiness. Is this how you are going to go about life as an adult? Shake it off and regain your self-respect.

If you respond with frustration, you wrap a strong cord tightly around the self-image and shrink it to the size of a small potato. Creativity is imprisoned inside, unable to come to your aid. Frustration is, in effect, the opposite of creativity. Frustration leads to dark depression. Creativity leads to bright discovery. If you find yourself frustrated with reoccurring objections, you must jab the self-image in its side. Tell yourself: "I am a clever, creative, experienced person capable of rising above these problems." Try this simple creativity exercise: for the objection that seems to derail your presentation, find not one but twenty answers. Get a blank sheet of paper and pencil and brainstorm every idea that comes to you to counter that objection. Don't judge your ideas; just write them all down. Also, write up a list of ten or twenty questions you could ask the prospect, to answer the objection with a provocative question rather than an answer. Put lots of options in front of you. Shake up your imagination.

If you respond with resentment, you must challenge yourself to be your biggest self, not your smallest self. Do you resent the idea that these clients and prospects have control over your career success? Think that through. Everybody has somebody with control over them. The President of the United States cannot achieve his agenda without securing the cooperation of members of Congress. Life is like the kids' game Scissors-Paper-Rock. Everybody is strongest one minute, weakest the next. There's no point in resenting the way of the world. I wonder if the person who gave his or her time to your meeting resents you for failing to satisfactorily solve the problems or meet his/her desires? You might be surprised. Do you resent some other salesperson in your office who seems to have an easier time of it? Even if that is true, how does directing your energy at him or her help you? Instead, rise to the challenge. Be the hero or heroine by making good under tough circumstances.

If you respond with dumb, stubborn persistence, you may get points for effort, but your family will starve! Unmitigated persistence is a vastly overrated characteristic. Oh, I believe in the power of persistence. In the early days of my practice, when day after day went by without so much as a phone call, and I had to wonder if I'd made a disastrous career mistake, I had to call upon all my faith just to get out of bed each morning. But if that first patient had not come, at some point, hopefully sooner than later, I would have applied my persistent energies to trying different ways of attracting patients and educating the public.

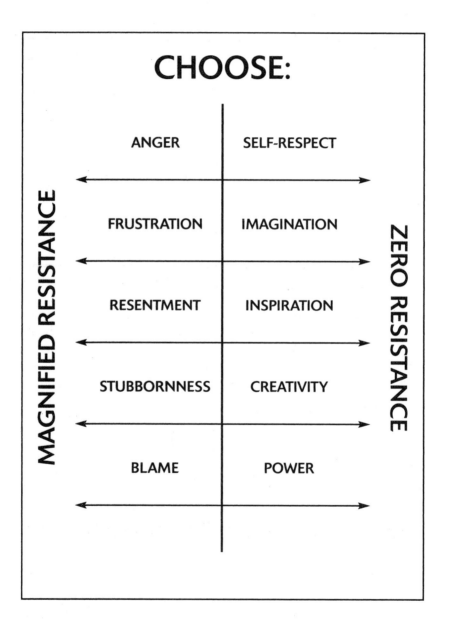

Have you ever seen a persistent golfer with a really terrible swing? Tight-lipped, tight-hipped, he lines up next to the ball, mutters at it under his breath, swings like a barn door on a broken hinge and sends the ball roaring off into the trees. What does he do next? Swings *harder*. The ball roars into the woods faster and disappears farther into oblivion. What does he do next? Swings even *harder*. This time he misses the ball altogether and wraps the club around himself. Believe me, swinging harder is just not the answer. Tackling the clients' objections you face by swinging harder is of little use either.

If you respond by blaming "the stupid customer," the terrible economy, the dirt-cheap competitors, or anyone else or anything else, you give up all your power. You accept helplessness. Your Success Mechanism rolls over and goes to sleep, for nothing is asked of it and there is no point to paying attention anymore. Your self-image shrinks, shrinks, shrinks.

Reason with yourself. If your customers are all fools and cheapskates, what does this say about you? If dirt-cheap competitors can make a better case for value than you, shouldn't this challenge you? Reason with yourself. You are paid to educate the customer, to develop and present the most persuasive case. The customer is not being paid to figure out why he or she should buy from you. If you place blame, you give up power. If you accept responsibility, you gain power.

Are you honest enough to see yourself in any of those scenarios? If you do, are you ready to do something about it? Can you see how you can take a little bit of resistance and magnify its power through your own emotional responses?

A Special Thought About Price Objections

At just about every sales convention or conference I ever spoke at and observed, there was at least one beat-up, bruised, struggling salesperson absolutely convinced that the only thing prospects cared about was the cheapest price.

Believe me, this is absolutely false. There is no place in America, even in the poorest areas; there is no group of people;

there is no industry or profession where everybody makes their buying decisions solely and purely based on cheapest price. If this were true, K-Mart would have put Nieman-Marcus out of business quite a few years ago. There would be no Cadillac dealerships. In my neighborhood in New York, there is a restaurant where you can get a great steak dinner for about $25. But right around the corner, there's another restaurant where you stand in line at the counter, serve yourself, and you can get a steak dinner—and I think the steak is just as tasty—for $9. How can these two restaurants both prosper?

I have given this a great deal of thought, and taken note of my own behavior, my friends' behavior, and my business clients' behavior when it comes to price. I find that everybody, myself included, loves a bargain but also understands value. Cheapest price seems to be the deciding factor in a purchase only when there is a simple commodity product involved, with no apparent value difference between one or another. Of course, this is the task of sales professionals: to persuasively present the value difference that favors their products.

One time when I was in a grocery store, I overheard a couple's discussion about cans of peas. The husband had put two cans of peas in the shopping cart. The wife put them back on the shelf and put two cans of a different brand of peas in their place. She patiently explained to her ill-informed husband that he had taken the cheapest peas, but that it was a generic brand, and that meant it was made with the poorest *quality* peas, rejected by the other brand name packagers, bought dirt-cheap by the packager of the generic products, etc. . . . That the cheap, generic peas would shrivel and shrink when cooked, . . . while the other brand, though costing a bit more, was made with good quality, plump, tasty peas, real butter, good spices and would make a much more satisfying side dish. "Sometimes," the woman said, "saving a few pennies just costs too much."

Now there is a statement every sales pro ought to memorize and add to their arsenal: "Sometimes saving a few pennies just costs too much!" This lady certainly knew how to overcome a price objection when it came to selling peas! Some salespeople I know could learn a thing or two from this smart shopper and persuasive spouse.

Why You Should Be Happy to Get Objections

May I suggest an entirely different viewpoint toward objections? Strategies and techniques for responding to objections are one thing, but an entire paradigm shift in your thinking about objections might be much more powerful.

You see, most salespeople see objections as resistance, to be feared, and when it occurs, to be resented. Instead let's look at selling as serving. Let's look at the process of getting to a closed sale as a partnership between you and your client. A team effort. *Partnership selling* is the wave of the future. Cooperation and conflict cannot exist in the same place at the same time. If you can focus on cooperation, you automatically vaporize conflict!

Consider these two mental movies:

Mental Movie Number One

You are a child again, out in your backyard on Easter morning, joyously engaged in the Easter egg and candy basket hunt. The Easter bunny—your parents, of course—have hidden big, foil-wrapped chocolate eggs, little baskets of tasty hard candies, colorfully painted hard-boiled eggs around the yard. See yourself in your T-shirt and shorts, rushing about, thrilled with the treasure hunt. As you move about, your parents call out "Cold. You're very cold."..."Warmer, you're getting warmer."..."Hot! You're really hot now!" What are they doing? Giving you clues to help you navigate the invisible maze and get to the treasures. Are they to be resented for this? Of course not. You welcome their clues. You need their help or you'll be out there all day.

Mental Movie Number Two:

You are a blind man trapped in a burning building. Danger is all around you, and time is of the essence. If you bumble about on your own, you will surely stumble and fall. A fireman finds you, takes your arm, and guides you through the smoldering, fallen timbers to the exit, where safety and fresh air are waiting. Do you get angry at him for interfering? Of course not. You embrace this man, who has just saved your life.

Now, back to this team effort of selling. When the customer gives you an objection, what is he doing? Stop seeing it as resistance! He is yelling out clues: *cold, warm, hot,* trying to let you know whether or not you are moving toward the successful sale and, if you are not, to alert you, so that you correct your course. With his questions and objections, he is the firefighter trying to guide you, zig-zagging around the dangers, to the goal. If you do not resist, there is no resistance; there is teamwork. This is wonderful!

This paradigm shift in the way that you see the process and the way you see objections will shake your Success Mechanism awake and inspire it to perform at its very best: bright, creative, resourceful, optimistic. Always remember that how you respond to and consciously think about a particular situation is "pulling the trigger" or "pushing the button" that activates either your Success Mechanism or Failure Mechanism.

How Objections Guarantee Job Security and Financial Rewards

I'll give you another reason to be happy you get objections. If there were no questions to be answered, objections to be overcome, or stalls to be conquered, you'd be driving a taxi cab for a living. If your clients sold themselves, why would your company need you?

For the most part, the universe rewards in proportion to difficulty. Diamond cutters are much better paid than meat cutters. Why? In large part because of the degree of difficulty of what they do. A surgeon is much better paid than a pharmacist. You have far more financial opportunity than the counter clerk at the corner convenience store or even the sales clerk at the department store cosmetics counter. Why? Because succeeding in your position is more difficult, challenging, and complex. Why is it so? Largely because your clients do not sell themselves; in your business, it is a team effort, requiring you to do a considerable amount of work.

Would you like a sales job where you never, never face a tough question or a challenging objection? Are you sure? Come with me to the ballpark and we'll get you the job of walking up and down the aisles selling peanuts, popcorn, and red-hots. No customer ever says: "I'm not sure I want a red-hot. Tell me about the ingredients and how it is made." Or "I'm thinking it over. Come back next week." Never. All you must do is yell at the top of your voice: "Peanuts! Popcorn! Red-hots! Get yer peanuts here!" and customers will pass money to you and buy. Unfortunately, you won't make $50,000 a year, have a company car or a corner office, or get much respect in this sales job.

When you look at the ladder of success in the selling field, you find these jobs where there are no objections raised and very little sales skill required at the bottom of the ladder. At the top of the income ladder, the sales positions requiring great skill, tact, knowledge, patience and confidence. These sales professionals deal with objections in almost every sale. Where would you prefer being on the ladder?

And I'll give you one more reason to welcome objections, for good measure. The questions, objections, and stalls you hear repeatedly represent *constructive* feedback, so you can correct your selling course, and experience greater success. It is far better to collect data and come to understand the chief reasons prospects say no to you than just to have them saying no but keeping their reasons a secret. This feedback is the raw material you must use to manufacture a stronger sales personality, a more convincing sales presentation.

Go into the Theater of Your Mind and try this little picture:

> You are seated comfortably at your desk. The door to your office opens and Ms. Stubborn Objection walks in. You greet her warmly with a smile, firm handshake, and invitation to be seated. "Thank you for coming in," you say sincerely, "I'm very happy that you are here. Now please give me all the information you can that will help me improve in selling." Then, as Ms. Stubborn Objection talks, you listen carefully, nondefensively, and jot down notes. Finally when she has exhausted herself, you escort her to the door and again thank her for coming in. "What a helpful woman," you say to yourself, "I'm happy she came in to share her ideas with me!"

How to Pre-Empt Objections

While I have just made a case for welcoming your prospects' objections with open arms, the ultimate goal is *pure* zero-resistance selling, including zero resistance from prospects. Is such a thing possible? Yes. There *are* sales professionals in just about every field who go through life, selling everyday, who rarely have an objection raised by their prospective clients. (This includes every one of this book's contributing authors!) And the fact that there are such pros says you can become one, too.

You can take certain steps to ensure that you only enter a selling situation where objections are very unlikely to occur at all. Regardless of what you sell, who you sell to, or what the norms seem to be in that field, I know that you can re-engineer the entire prospecting, selling, and closing process as well as your own attitudes, so that resistance virtually disappears.

Presuming you are in front of the correct prospect in the first place, then the reasons for objections occurring are limited to 1) Poor positioning, or 2) unconvincing presentation.

Positioning has to do with how you are perceived by your prospects; in a way, it is your self-image projected and made tangible and physical.

I recall, early in my lecture career, overhearing several salesmen talking outside the auditorium, before I was to speak. One said to the others: "Just what we need, another damned motivational speaker."

Oh-oh, I said to myself, that is *not* how I need to be positioned! I later went to great pains to be presented as a distinguished medical doctor who had made breakthrough discoveries about the human mind, written a best-selling book on his findings, used his findings to help top athletes improve their performance, and occasionally lectured on his techniques. I capitalized on the good fortune I had to have a number of celebrities read my book and contact me as a result, like the great artist Salvador Dali or the champion golfer Dave Stockton, among others. I wrapped the cloak of celebrity around my shoulders, too. I sought newspaper and magazine publicity for my research, my book, my lectures and myself.

When Maltz came to talk, it was not "just another speaker," it was an event. I did not see myself as "just another speaker" so I did not let the world view me that way either.

I assure you: you do not want to be perceived as "just another damned salesman" either. *Stature melts away resistance.* Now this is a very important statement, and you ought to give it some very serious thought. *You* must determine your own stature in the world. You must decide what you are—other than "just another salesman"—and then project that to your clientele and community.

In 1960, my ideas about human behavior were radical and revolutionary. Had someone without credentials and an aura of expertise talked about these ideas from the platform, in a seminar, he or she would have been ignored or laughed at, and would have had no impact. Because I emphasized my credentials as a medical doctor and a man of science, presented my ideas as discoveries made through my work with thousands of patients, and linked my ideas to the developing guided-missile technology (cybernetics in action), I was able to command attention and respect. My stature melted away a lot of resistance.

If a farmer in Iowa reports seeing a spaceship hovering above his fields, most people ignore him or laugh at him. But if a former astronaut, now a jet test pilot, with 20 years experience in the U.S. Air Force and in NASA, reports seeing a spaceship flying at the wing tip of his plane for several miles, then hovering above a town below, a lot of people think long and hard about it. What's the difference? Stature.

How do you, a salesperson, gain stature in the eyes of your prospects? This is a very smart question to ponder. Stature is a heated butter knife that easily melts resistance, so it is something you definitely want to have! I don't know your particular circumstances, but maybe you can write and publish books or articles, give lectures, get publicity in industry magazines, obtain certified credentials, be recognized for exceptional achievements, or gain the endorsements of celebrity customers or clients known to everybody in a given industry. One financial planner I know hosts his own radio call-in show. And a carpet cleaner gets her credentials from a technical training institute. All real estate salespeople are number one in some category. If a doctor can write a book on weight loss, a printing salesman distribute an audio cassette every month on which he interviews experts on advertising, direct-mail, and marketing, *you* can use your imagination to find opportunities to stand out from the crowd and be recognized for your knowledge, expertise, leadership and service. You can develop your stature *strategically*.

When your prospect views you as a cut above ordinary salespeople in your field, he is more likely to accept your recommendations, less likely to object, less likely to resist.

Four Keys to Delivering a Convincing Presentation

A truly convincing presentation can melt away all remaining resistance like the hot summer sun melting a frozen ice cream pop right off of its stick. Here are four keys to delivering a convincing presentation:

1. *A healthy, vibrant, strong self-image.* You see yourself as a knowledgeable professional providing real value to your clients, deserving of their confidence and trust, and deserving of rich rewards for your efforts.

2. *Legitimate confidence in your products or services.* You know that what you offer is superior to other alternatives in important ways, is a good value for your client, and is praised by those customers already benefiting from it.

3. *Legitimate confidence in yourself.* This is the kind of confidence that comes from competence. You have good communication skills, a pleasant, effective personality, good listening skills; in other words, you know how to sell. And you have a solid, persuasive, practiced (though not canned) presentation.

4. *Honest enthusiasm.* Not the fake kind that is outside of your own personality, but genuine enthusiasm based on enjoying selling, enjoying meeting with people, enjoying solving clients' problems.

If this describes you, you are equipped to deliver convincing presentations. If this does not describe you, then do something about it. If you need to strengthen your self-image, by all means, dig into *Psycho-Cybernetics* and do so. In addition to this and the other books on the subject available at your bookstore, there is a 12-week programmed home study course specifically for this purpose, available from the foundation.

If you lack confidence in the superior value of your products, you must either obtain the added knowledge you need to develop such unshakable confidence or have the integrity to go find something else to sell that you can wholeheartedly believe in. Selling without integrity forces you to rely on unfairly manipulative, "hard sell" tactics, and will eat away at your self-image until it is gnawed full of painful holes.

If you lack fundamental selling competence, there are abundant opportunities to remedy that. For general communication skills, you can't beat the Dale Carnegie Course. It is offered in most areas and you can find it in your local telephone directories.

To learn a complete selling system, consider assistance offered by The Brooks Group. Also, be sure to use mental rehearsal to fine-tune your sales presentations.

Four Keys to Delivering a Convincing Presentation

Key #1:   A vibrant, healthy, strong self-image

Key #2:   Legitimate confidence in your products and services

Key #3:   Legitimate confidence in yourself

Key #4:   Honest enthusiasm

Do not permit your ego to get in your way here. It may insist that you already know everything you need to know to sell. It will tell you that you are "above" taking some sales course or seminar or otherwise seeking additional education. Yet, I've rarely met a "know-it-all" who is number one in his/her sales organization. Most sales professionals develop skill strengths and weaknesses over time. Just about everybody has great competence in some aspects of selling but may barely get by in other aspects. Be honest with yourself about your strengths and weaknesses, and take constructive action to reduce your weaknesses.

Six Building Blocks of a Convincing Presentation

Once you are equipped to deliver your presentation, the following key ingredients will ensure your success:

1. Diagnosis. Before or at the presentation, you must do as I did as a doctor: diagnose. You can't just rush in like a bull in a China shop touting the exact same solution for everyone. How would you feel about a doctor who only talked about back surgery to every patient who came through his door regardless of their ailments? The prospect has to see and believe that you are evaluating his/her particular needs and desires. I'd bet that at least half of all the people who came to me asking for help began their discussion with "Doctor, my problem is unique." Of course, it rarely was. But they believed it was. And I would have lost my effectiveness with them if I had, in any way, indicated that I thought it wasn't unique. You cannot afford to become blasé about your clients' situations.

2. Customization. You use the information collected in diagnosis to customize your basic, practiced, reliable presentation to each individual prospect. I am a strong believer in mentally rehearsed presentations, but *not* in delivering the same "canned" presentation to each prospect. What is the difference? The top pro takes carefully crafted, well-rehearsed and practiced presentation content he/she has confidence in and integrates it with information obtained through research and diagnosis. No two presentations are the same, yet in some ways, every presentation is the same.

Speakers use this same strategy. Every time I spoke to a group about Psycho-Cybernetics, I used many of the same stories and illustrations, and I certainly endeavored to convey the same fundamental principles. I used enough proven material that I had great confidence in to feel confident and comfortable at the podium. But I also took care to weave in what I learned in advance about the particular audience, current events, local events, and other one-of-a-kind items into my presentation.

3. Honesty. Resistance really melts away when your client senses and is confident that you are telling the truth about your products and services, your company, and your own expertise.

Many salespeople err, for example, by hiding the flaw in their product. They never mention it, and they hope the prospect doesn't. They are distracted throughout their presentation, sweating this out; will she or won't she notice? This is a huge mistake. It is far better to acknowledge the flaw and counter it as best you can. The stature you gain with your prospect and with your own self-image by telling the truth is enormous.

4. *Value.* Here's a little mental movie to illustrate how value determines whether or not there will be objections, especially price objections:

> Inside your prospect's head, there is a good-sized, gold-plated balance scale. There are two laborers there, to load things on to the scales. On the ground in front of the scale, there are two piles of one pound concrete blocks. All of the ones in the pile on the left are painted bright green and labeled "Value." All the ones on the right side are painted bright red and labeled "Cost." Green means "Go!" Red means "Stop!" All the while you are talking with your prospect, these two laborers are responding to his/her thoughts by putting concrete blocks onto the scales. If he or she accepts a benefit, a green block, maybe even two or three get loaded onto the left side of the scale. If he/she is unconvinced of a benefit or a benefit is unimportant to him/her, a red block goes on to the right side of the scale. When all is said and done, the scale is tilted either to the left to "Go!" or to the right to "Stop!" by the weight of the concrete blocks.

It's your job to have so much more weight on the green side than on the red that all the prospect wants to do is grab your offer quick, before you change your mind! To me, when value overwhelmingly, irresistibly, inarguably and clearly outweighs cost, I buy. Keep in mind, of course, there is "emotional value" as well as "logical value" involved in every sale.

Not long ago, I bought a new Burberry overcoat. Quite honestly, I paid more for this coat than for any coat I've ever bought in my life. By most standards, I paid too much. But the sales clerk pointed out the fine quality double stitching; the extra inside, oversize pockets with zipper closures to prevent my loss of a passport or airline tickets or important papers; the extra large collar to turn up in winter winds; and the fact that a Burberry is made so well it will outlast three or four ordinary overcoats. Each time she made one of these points, a green brick plopped onto the Go side of the Value Scale. She also pointed out how handsome I looked in the coat, in the three-way mirror. She noted that an important doctor and author like me deserved the best overcoat money could buy. She even said that when I took the coat off and anyone I was with, perhaps doing business with, noticed the Burberry label, they would instantly know I was a man of class and distinction. More green bricks. The first batch from logic, the second from emotion. Finally she pointed out that the store was running a special promotion, so I could pick out a scarf free with my coat. I confess I did not even ask the price or look at the price tag before saying "I'll take this one."

5. *Proof.* These days, we live in a skeptical and cynical world. A lot of resistance exists because people automatically have their guard up all the time. It's smart to have plenty of good evidence to support every claim or promise you make. Here are some very good rules about proof:

- Rule 1: Never make a claim you cannot support with proof. I suppose every salesperson is tempted to exaggerate, to stretch the truth, from time to time. You might get away with it, but the damage doing so does to your self-image far outweighs the temporary, situational gain.

- Rule 2: When you can support a claim with proof, by all means do so. One promise proved is more powerful than a hundred unsupported promises.

- Rule 3: Keep updating your evidence. Be sure to read the periodicals of your industry, your newest company literature, general business and consumer magazines, and a daily newspaper. Be alert for facts, scientific studies, anecdotes involving famous people, and other information you can use to prove your selling points.

- Rule 4: Err in using too much proof rather than in using too little. If you were prosecuting a deadly serial killer, and you had a dozen witnesses with vivid, detailed testimony about the killer's evil behavior, would you call only three and leave nine on the shelf, to speed up the trial?

- Rule 5: Only use proof you know to be valid, honest and that you personally have confidence in.

6. Pictures. The use of pictures speeds up the convincing process. In cosmetic surgery, before-and-after pictures are almost universally used. In chiropractic, the patient's own X-rays are used, often placed side by side on a light box with X-rays of a healthy spine, to convince the patient of the need for care. In industrial selling, it's increasingly common to use videotapes, to show equipment in use, differences in wear and tear of parts, even testimonials from customers. And late night TV is overrun with infomercials; in many cases, half-hour long sequences of very visual, dramatic product demonstrations. Why are all these pictures so powerful? Because most people think in pictures.

You can also use words to create pictures. It's very powerful to start a sentence with "Imagine" or "Picture this." I once heard a top salesman of copiers and other office equipment say: "Picture this: the line of people wasting time, standing in line to use the copier is gone, because this model is four times faster than yours, has six auto-set and walk away modes, and can even be networked into the desktop computers."

Six Building Blocks of a Convincing Presentation

#1: Diagnosis

#2: Customization

#3: Honesty

#4: Value

#5: Proof

#6: Pictures

The Ultimate Secret for Eliminating Stalls and Objections Before They Happen

A number of people who have thoroughly studied top performers in selling, incredibly charismatic and persuasive people, have arrived at the conclusion that these individuals somehow "transmit" their ideas to the other person or people nonverbally, directly to the subconscious rather than through the conscious mind. Some people call this extrasensory perception or ESP. The famous Kreskin frequently goes on talk shows or holds public demonstrations, where he is able to "pick up" the unspoken thoughts of others and to "send" his unspoken thoughts into others' minds. While much of Kreskin's act is showmanship and the equal of the magician's sleight of hand, too many respected men and women have experienced this sort of thing and come to believe in it, and there is too much positive evidence to ignore. Kreskin himself insists that everybody has some level of this ability in them, and that they can deliberately develop more. Inventors like Thomas Edison, authors like Napoleon Hill and Dr. Edward Kramer, and successful entrepreneurs like Conrad Hilton have all written of their experiences in "sending" or "receiving" messages.

Do I believe that, as a salesperson, you can "send" messages directly into the subconscious mind of your prospect and, by doing so, influence his/her behavior? Well, yes and no.

I am reluctant to buy into the mystical. What I do believe is that we communicate on many different levels, in many different ways, both verbally and nonverbally. Through our eyes, for instance. We think, consciously, mostly about how we communicate by speaking, and we pretty much leave the other ways to themselves. It's my contention that when you hold a very strong, confident, vivid image of successful outcome in your mind, that directs your Servo-Mechanism to create the right body language and nonverbal communication, to show the right feeling in your eyes, to put the right tonality and inflection in your voice.

The face and the eyes definitely deliver messages. Humans are capable of as many as 20,000 different facial expressions. Imagine that: 20,000 different facial expressions, each communicating, revealing a slightly different message.

How can you control the message sent by your eyes, face, body language? The biggest secret is that picture you hold inside your own mind. Your "inside" controls the "outside."

When we say that prospects sense your own uncertainty or anxiety, they are actually receiving that message through a combination of these things, like posture, gestures, or voice tone. When the Servo-Mechanism is targeted properly, it guides you in all these areas, so you "send" and the prospect "receives" the right message.

By using the Psycho-Cybernetic Techniques described in this chapter, you can be certain of sending the message that will melt away resistance and help you close sales easily.

Chapter 3

Selling Successfully When You're in Over Your Head

You've worked very hard to get this opportunity, but this morning, as you looked at yourself in the mirror, the reality of what you are up against really hit home. Maybe it would be better for one of the more experienced account execs to handle this presentation. After all, what makes you think you're up to this, anyway? You've never landed an account even half this size. The conference room you'll be meeting in will probably be as big as your whole apartment! The prospect's custom-made suit worth more than all the furniture in your apartment! You feel your planned and rehearsed comments disappearing from memory, your anxiety rising. The face in the mirror says: buddy, it looks like you've bitten off more than you can chew!

Sales professionals perform under pressure all the time. Some people are thwarted by the challenges of instant feedback, possibility of rejection, and compensation directly linked to performance. Some people thrive on these challenges. But even the best salesperson will, from time to time, feel thrust into a situation where he or she is overmatched. Even the best sales pro may be intimidated or fearful of the presentation to the really "big" prospect.

This is just one more thing that sales professionals and athletes share; the need to successfully manage, even to thrive under extraordinary pressure.

Consider the following article from *USA Today* (8/8/96):

A few days before the Olympic decathlon, Dan O'Brien was in a familiar place, but he knew he couldn't stay. "Dan admitted he was having trouble sleeping," sports psychologist Jim Reardon says. "He couldn't shut his mind down. He was thinking things like: 'what if I don't win? What if this happens? What if that happens?'"

In 1992, O'Brien didn't qualify for the U.S. Olympic team.

So Reardon went into action. "We talked about refocusing," he says. "We did some progressive muscle relaxation, focused on breathing and replaced negative thoughts with positive thoughts."

Sports psychology, the art of enhancing mental skills to reach physical goals, is being heralded by athletes as the performance revolution of the 1990's. . . .

"I'm a much better athlete, much more aware of myself," O'Brien says. "I know what kind of feelings I'm going through. And I know how to cope with these feelings before they hurt my performance."

Think about this: sports are physical, very physical, yet athletes are increasingly embracing mental training as the key to success. You may feel that selling is technical, a sequence of steps and applied techniques. But top salespeople are increasingly embracing mental training as their key to success.

In a sense, athletes like Dan O'Brien are "in over their head" every time they compete. The other athletes they face are at least physical equivalents if not superior. The talent level at the very top of every sport, in the amateur and in the pro ranks, is simply awesome. And these people perform in high-pressure, make-it-or-break-it situations constantly, often under the critical scrutiny of thousands, tens of thousands, or—thanks to TV—millions of observers. Think of the "comeback kings" of pro football like Fran Tarkenton or John Elway. How can Elway stay so cool, calm, purposeful and focused with only a few ticks remaining on the clock, the roar of 60,000 people around him, the noise on the field, the rushing defense, and the need to score or be out of the play-offs?

This is what we often call the "money player" in sports. The fellow who can make that million dollar putt and wrestle the tournament championship away from the elder statesmen, the old pros of the game. Or the second-string quarterback who comes off the bench late in the game and can bring a team back from a great point deficit, under pressure of a diminishing clock, time running out, and blitzes by the defenders.

The true money player in sports is able to sustain peak performance even under enormous pressure, even in the most disadvantageous of conditions.

In that same *USA Today* article, Jason Elam, the Denver Broncos' all-star place kicker talked about using relaxation and visualization drills to prepare for a game. In 1995, Elam made all 39 of his extra point attempts, 31 of 38 field goal attempts, and scored 132 points. His sports psychologist says that "the vast majority are not using it to solve a problem but to tap into the vast power of the mind to reach higher levels of achievement."

Would you like to have the calm confidence of an Elway or Elam? I believe this is within reach of every sales professional. You can condition your self-image to make you a "money player" in selling!

Even If You Are "Outclassed," You Can Still Win

How do you know when you are in over your head? I'm told that racehorses can look each other in the eye and sense "class" differences. Often, the horse of lower class may be fast enough to beat the horse of higher class, may draw up next to him, but will not pass him! Certainly, one group of athletes can look at their own strengths, weaknesses, and statistics and compare themselves to their opponents and tell whether or not they are in over their heads. Does a lower class ever beat a higher class horse? Yes. Not the majority of times, but often enough to invalidate class as a primary handicapping method. Does a technically inferior team ever beat a significantly superior team? Yes. Not the majority of times, but often enough to invalidate superiority-on-paper, statistical comparisons, as the way to predict outcomes of games.

People quite often get in over their heads and still emerge victorious. I have long been fascinated by this; by the individual who is clearly outclassed in some contest, competition or situation, yet rises above that disadvantage and still wins. The self-image of such a person is worthy of study by any sales professional seeking peak performance even in apparently difficult selling situations.

Early in my writing and speaking about Psycho-Cybernetics, I spent some time with a most unusual man. As an entrepreneur, he had taken over a virtually bankrupt, troubled chain of stores and turned them into a giant, thriving retail empire in a few short years. For a while, an article predicting the death of this company or criticizing him as either a brutal axe-wielder, eliminating jobs and ruining lives, or a cutthroat deal-maker appeared in the newspapers just about every day. The bankers all turned their back on this guy, and he had to secure financing from overseas sources. At the same time this man was in the middle of this business storm, his personal life was also in chaos. His wife was divorcing him, it was messy, and the ugly details made their way into the society pages as well as the tabloids. On top of all this, he was also under indictment for securities fraud, related to another business deal. I asked him how he was able to deal with all these problems at the same time and still keep his eye on the ball and get things done.

> "I've always been the kind of person who can stand up to criticism and crisis. I'm not really bothered by being surrounded by problems and critics. I know I'll ultimately prevail. My whole life, I've been getting truckloads of shit dumped on me and coming out of the pile smelling like a rose."

I don't know if he was aware of it or not, but he answered my question with a very clear, powerful, dynamic *Self-Image Programming Statement.* He described a self-image that just doesn't acknowledge the possibility of failure. If we look inside your self-image, and see what's there having to do with crisis or criticism, what would we find?

Are You a Goat Or a Tiger?

Consider the Oriental fable about the little tiger orphaned immediately after birth, raised by a friendly herd of goats. The little tiger played with the goat kids, drank milk from the nanny goat, and slept secure in the goat's cave. Quite naturally, the little fellow came to think of himself as a goat. He did his best to bleat like a goat. He tried to cultivate a taste for grass and paper.

One day a huge Bengal tiger came bounding into the clearing where the little tiger was playing with the goats. As the tiger roared, the goats ran for cover. The little tiger was the only "goat" who didn't race away. Instead, he felt strangely drawn to the huge, magnificent creature.

The big tiger led the little fellow down the hill to a nearby river and urged him to take a close look at his reflection in the water. Whenever he had looked in the water before, he had seen his reflection as an odd-looking goat, because that was what he expected to see. But now he saw his reflection differently, as a tiger.

The big tiger let out a tree-shaking roar. "Why don't you roar like that?" "Never tried," thought the little tiger. He sat back on his haunches like the big tiger did, took a deep breath, and tried to roar. To his surprise, he felt a rumble deep within his stomach. It grew stronger. He opened his mouth wide and the most amazing roar came out, cascading over the jungle. From that day forward he knew he could never be a goat again.

You can be a tiger, not a goat. A lion, not a mouse. Your big self, not your small self. You may never have tried to roar, and that's all there is to it. If you feel you are in over your head, you probably aren't. You've probably just never tried going there before. Most people have more talent and ability than they give themselves credit for. Go ahead and throw back your head and roar as loudly as you can. You'll probably surprise yourself!

Why You Should Put Out the Welcome Mat for "Fear"

When you fear an impending selling situation, and feel that you may be in over your head, what is really going on? Such fear is a sign that you are growing and stretching and pushing against your comfort zone, and that is a very healthy and potentially rewarding thing to do. The fear feeling tells you that you are succeeding at getting your instructions to your Servo-Mechanism. The fear feeling is a way your Servo-Mechanism checks an instruction it's not familiar with; it's like the Servo-Mechanism saying, "Hey, are you sure you want to do this?"

Well, there's nothing wrong with that. You must then respond emphatically, definitively, and forcefully: "Yes, that is exactly what I intend to do. You heard me right. Now get that Success Mechanism of ours up, out of bed, give it a cup of coffee, and get it to work."

You Are *Not* Your Fears

The fear feeling is a natural, temporary response to unfamiliar and uncomfortable instructions you send to your Servo-Mechanism. But you are separate from your fear; you and your fear feeling are not one in the same. You can honestly acknowledge that you feel fear about doing a particular thing but then go ahead and do it anyway, and most of the time, the fear feeling will be dissolved by the action.

There is an old proverb: "Fear and doubt knocked on the door. Faith and courage answered. There was no one there."

Every Coin Has Two Sides

In the *Batman* comic books (and in one of the recent *Batman* movies), there is a villain called "Two Face." One side of his face is horribly scarred and disfigured, the other handsome. One side of his personality is evil, dark, twisted and violent; the other decent and compassionate. To determine which side of his personality to let loose in a situation, and decide whether to let an adversary live or die, he flips a two-faced coin.

While this is an interesting character study, Two Face is certainly not a model to emulate. Surely you do not want to leave your personality or the outcome of the day to the flip of a coin! Yet, every one of our self-images *does* have two faces: the *Automatic Success*

Mechanism (ASM) and the *Automatic Failure Mechanism* (AFM). You do not need to flip a coin to choose which one to let loose and which one to lock up. The choice should be obvious, and therefore, conscious and deliberate.

Unfortunately, most people go through life letting the ASM or the AFM loose pretty much at random, sometimes provoked by incidents or other people. But rarely, deliberately chosen. Also, in most peoples' lives, the AFM grows stronger and more dominant with the passage of time.

Given the opportunity, your ASM can be counted on to help you rise up and excel in a high-pressure situation, to find the opportunity concealed in crisis; to be strong, not weak. Conversely, given the opportunity, your AFM can be counted on to sabotage you in high-pressure situations, to be overwhelmed in a crisis; to be weak, not strong.

Picture in your mind two giant light switches mounted on the side of a huge computer: your Servo-Mechanism. One is a red switch, which can turn on or turn off your Failure Mechanism. The other is a green switch, which can turn on or off your Success Mechanism. As you face high-pressure selling situations, here are some tips for flipping the green switch *on* and the red switch *off*:

1. Use the Theater of Your Mind. Sit down, get comfortable and replay mental movies of times in your life when you have performed well under pressure. Of times in your career when you have successfully won over an especially tough prospect, closed an especially large or important sale, or otherwise excelled at selling when you felt in over your head. Relive these experiences.

2. Enrich your professional image. Wear your very best business attire and keep it cleaned, pressed, and neat. Dress each morning as if you were going to meet with the President of the United States. Use good business tools, including a quality pen. Carry a quality briefcase. Present a successful outer image to the world at large, so you can present a successful self-image to yourself.

3. Use affirmations. Write out and frequently read or recite strong Self-Image Programming Statements.

4. Use visual psychological triggers to remind yourself of your ambitions and abilities. These can be affirmations written out on large cards, photographs, or objects that have instant meaning to you. A photo of an athlete who performs well under pressure and whom you admire can trigger thoughts of "calm under pressure." A giant clock might be a trigger for "do it now."

5. Acquire new skills or fine-tune your present skills. Build competence to build confidence.

6. Prepare. If you are going to meet with Mr. High-tech, a very important prospect, learn what you can about him and his company. If he has been written about in the media, get to the library and read those articles. If he has written a book, read it. If somebody you know well knows him, go or call and get his impressions. Give yourself the edge of understanding as much as you can about the person, his or her business, or industry.

7. Go into the Theater of Your Mind and mentally rehearse the perfect sales presentation. Put the prospect into your movie, script lines and have him or her deliver them, ably respond to questions, establish rapport, and make astute suggestions the prospect is impressed with. Picture him or her growing more enthusiastic as the meeting goes on. See the sale being completed with ease. After you have constructed this scenario, rehearse it over and over again. When the actual meeting rolls around, it'll feel like deja vu.

8. Do not give your mind time to manufacture undue anxiety. Do not make the mistake of sitting around idle the day before, evening before, or morning of the "big presentation." Stick to your typical activities. Be productive.

A Look at a Sales Pro in Over His Head

After giving a speech to a big sales group, I was pulled aside by a man who had been sitting in the front row. I had noticed him while giving my speech because he had seemed distracted the entire hour. Now he said, "Dr. Maltz, I really need your advice in private.

Can you please give me a few minutes of your time?" We ducked into an unoccupied meeting room next door, found a couple chairs and sat down across from one another.

MM: Okay, Tom, what's on your mind?

TOM: I'm very nervous about this presentation I'm going to make next week. The prospect is a multimillionaire, a highly successful entrepreneur. You read about him in *Business Week* and *Fortune*. And here I am, running a small, three-man computer firm, with no big clients to brag about. This guy makes more money in a month than our whole firm does in a year. And I hear he's one tough cookie to deal with. I'm afraid he's going to eat me up and spit me out.

MM: Well, that's a lot to deal with. Let's take your concerns apart and discuss them one at a time, okay?

TOM: Okay.

MM: Tell me how you got this appointment with this very important CEO in the first place.

TOM: It's incredible. A friend of his bought a copy of my book in the bookstore, gave to him, and he had his secretary call me. Apparently they are having problems with computer networks and employee utilization, and in my book, I talk a lot about the futility of technology if not accepted and embraced by people. I'm sort of an expert in integrating new communication technology into corporate environments.

MM: So you're an author. Has this CEO written a book?

TOM: Well, no, I don't think so.

MM: I've written a book too. I find that a lot of people look up to authors. They admire us for having the tenacity to complete a book and get it published. And they see us as top experts because of our books. Do you think it's possible that this man admires you because you are a published author?

TOM: I don't know. It never occurred to me.

MM: Well, he has sought you out because you are an expert in a highly specialized field, right? And presumably he has no one on his staff with your expertise, right?

TOM: Yes, I'd assume that's right.

MM: But you are intimidated because he makes a lot more money than you do and is wealthier than you are.

TOM: Yes.

MM: Do you think he has his children enrolled in a private school?

TOM: I'd think so. With all his money, they're probably in the best prep school in the country.

MM: And what do you think the teachers at that prep school earn as a year's salary?

TOM: Well, maybe $40,000 or so.

MM: A lot less than your CEO! And what do you think the dean of that prep school earns? A lot less than the CEO. But that doesn't stop him from choosing those experts to educate his children. Does he have a private plane?

TOM: The company has two jets.

MM: And what do you think the pilots make working for him?

TOM: I have no idea. Maybe $70,000?

MM: Well, a lot less than he does. But that doesn't stop him from putting his life in that pilot's hands, does it?

TOM: I'm getting the idea.

MM: Of course! An astute, successful man like this must choose the people who make his success possible based on many different criteria, not just by how much they earn. You see, when you compare yourself to someone else's best, in their area of expertise, you can't win and you shrink your self-image to the size of a small potato. His area of expertise is making money. But yours is getting people to embrace technology to boost productivity. If he compares himself to you in that arena, he's the guaranteed loser. If I compare myself to Arnold Palmer on the golf course, I lose. I am in awe of what Palmer can do on the golf course. But if Arnold Palmer compares himself to me in plastic surgery, he loses. He'd be in awe of what I can do with a scalpel. You need take a back seat to no man because you have developed specialized expertise that has put you in demand, garnered respect of colleagues and clients alike, and has brought an important CEO like this man to your doorstep, looking to you for help.

TOM: That's a very different way of looking at things than what I had been thinking.

MM: Can you find fault with it?

TOM: Not really.

MM: Good. Now what about this man's reputation as a tough cookie. What are you, a marshmallow? I'm betting he has to be tough-minded. When you control the kind of money he does, the line of con artists, charlatans, greedy and selfish trying to get it must be very long. This man knows how to separate those who know their stuff from the pretenders. Now, is that good or bad for you?

TOM: Well, I sure know my stuff.

MM: That, my friend, is the ticket. Your self-image is strong and healthy because you are a legitimate expert who can deliver on your promises. Is there any question about this topic you cannot handle?

TOM: Not that I know of.

MM: Then what do you have to fear from someone likely to ask the very smartest and best questions you've ever been asked? Here is a marvelous opportunity to demonstrate your skills to someone capable not only of rewarding you with a big contract but also introducing you to other top CEOs, so you can take your company to the next level. Is fear the most appropriate response?

TOM: I guess not. But you can certainly understand why I would worry about screwing this up.

MM: Yes and no. I understand how important this is. But you have four days to prepare. Not worry, prepare. Here is my prescription: go home and write down on a pad every question he might raise. Put yourself in his shoes. Be tough-minded, even abrasive, cynical and suspicious. Put yourself on the hot seat. Then determine what your answers are to all these questions. Go into the Theater of the Mind and put it all together as a vividly detailed mental movie in which you are the conquering hero, as you should be based on your expertise. See yourself responding to his toughest questions coolly and calmly. See yourself winning his respect. Get this movie right, then rerun it a dozen times a day. Rehearse this perfect interview. When the real thing occurs, it'll be deja vu. And it'll probably be easier in reality than you make it in your mind, you can look forward to that. I also want you to separately create a picture of this CEO, with all the money in the world, but vexed everyday by these problems that you can solve, tossing and turning at night because of this frustration. See him hollering madly: "My kingdom for a solution to this problem!" See the relief on his face and in his mind when he realizes you can get this nagging aggravation out of his life once and for all. This is the fellow you are going to meet with and bond with.

TOM: I'll do it!

MM: Good. And be sure to let me know how things turn out. I'll be expecting good news.

As you might assume, I later got a call from a triumphant Tom. He had been well received by his very important prospect, delivered a powerful presentation, and secured the account with virtually zero resistance. If Tom ever feels like he is in over his head again, he'll be able to recall this actual experience and remind his self-image that he is the kind of sales pro who rises to the occasion and performs successfully under pressure.

If you feel in over your head, you can go into the Theater of Your Mind, sit down across from me, and we can have a conversation similar to the one Tom and I had. You see, by the time you've finished this book, you'll understand how I would react and what I would say in just about any situation, so you can make me come and join you for a little coaching session anytime you like.

Why Did You Come Into This World?

Did the miracle of human life occur in your case so that you could someday grow up, face a big and important opportunity, and fail? Of course not! My friend, you came into this world *to succeed*. I believe that as certainly as I believe in the law of gravity. And if this is so, you can rest assured that you will not be placed face-to-face with an opportunity or challenge too big for you to handle. If you think, even for a second, that you are in over your head, you must remind yourself that you came into this world to succeed and that you are now presented with this situation because you are ready for it.

There is one kind of selling you must never do, and that is: sell yourself short. Dr. Abraham Maslow noted that the history of humankind is rife with people selling themselves short. My own observation is that the history of humankind is full of inspiring instances of men and women of all ages and backgrounds rising up to excel against the apparent odds, to face extraordinary challenges and rise above them to success.

Too many people grow up with the idea that they have come into this world for some purpose other than to succeed at every worthwhile endeavor they apply themselves to—but why? Some people seem to think they were born to suffer, yet this cannot be justified. How perverse would a Creator have to be, to assemble a world as full of opportunity as this, and then place a person in it destined to fail? Some people tell their self-images that they were "born to lose." Then they are their own perverse creators, condemning themselves to hell on earth.

The truth is that you are never in over your head! You came into this world to succeed. No opportunity appears before you that you are not more than equipped to handle masterfully. No person is your superior. You are unique. Remind yourself of these great truths when you face a challenge in selling and you will rise above it to success!

Mastering Tough Selling Situations

There are a number of critical selling situations in which people often feel they are in over their head. Here are a few ideas on how to handle them.

Multilevel or Network Marketing

Estimates vary, but there seems to be at least 10 million people, roughly 5% of the United States population, and millions more abroad involved in *network marketing*. Most are part time, with the dual role of selling products to consumers and recruiting, training and motivating others to join the business, who will in turn, sell and recruit. This unusual approach to distributing products and providing opportunities has built a number of giant corporate empires, helped hundreds of thousands of people create substantial incomes with no investment other than effort, and provided a training ground for others, who gain confidence and skills they later use to succeed in other endeavors.

If you are in network marketing, then you already know it falls into the category of "easier said than done." There are emotional, psychological and practical obstacles to conquer in achieving success in this unusual business.

Todd Smith is a leading distributor in one of these network marketing companies. He has been featured in magazines, interviewed on radio and television, and recognized throughout the network marketing industry for his flair for this business. Last year, his personal income exceeded 1.8 million dollars. That's enough to get my attention! I buy that Todd understands how to succeed in this type of business.

Todd says that most people who are attracted to network marketing are introverts, not extroverts, so as soon as they've used up their "warm market" of family, close friends and neighbors, they begin experiencing great difficulty acquiring additional customers or recruiting more distributors. For most of these people, this is like smacking right up against a brick wall!

This is the reason why most network marketing companies feature highly consumable products, so each person's cadre of few customers buys again and again. This is also the reason why most network marketing companies' compensation plans allow a person with only a few personally recruited people to still profit based on the depth—not the breadth—of his or her organization. It also explains these organizations' increasing preference for using what you might call introverted sales methods, such as handing out or mailing out cassette tapes that tell the sales story for the distributor.

It's obvious to me, and probably to you, if you're in one of these businesses, that the introvert could benefit enormously by becoming less so, and becoming more outgoing, assertive and persuasive. If you stop to think about it, each person who joins a network marketing organization brings with him- or herself a self-image that isn't "up to speed."

For instance, one day a fellow is a working stiff. He goes to his job every morning, goes through the routine of fastening fasteners on an assembly line or processing paperwork in an office, goes home, eats dinner, and watches TV or plays a game with his children. He probably feels reasonably content with his life. He and his wife get the bills paid, are buying their house, and have pretty much suppressed any youthful dreams of wealth, mansions or travel to exotic ports. His self-image has accepted all that. His self-image is that of an ordinary, average fellow. Now, all of a sudden, a tape plops into his lap or a friend takes him to an "opportunity meeting" and—wham!—his aspirations and goals change overnight. Now he wants a bigger income, a new car, money in the bank, a business of his own, pride, and respect. His self-image hasn't a chance to catch up. It's woken abruptly to find this guy attempting to do things it knows he has no business doing.

"What is this all about?" grumbles the self-image. "Hey, you, wait a minute," it hollers. "What on earth makes you think you're a salesman? You've never sold anything in your life! Heck, your parents had to buy 144 candy bars once when you were supposed to be selling them to raise money for a band trip in high school."

Maybe this fellow defies his self-image and makes a sale or two.

"Whoa," yells his self-image. "Don't you remember being told not to talk to strangers? You got by with this sales thing with your friends because they felt obligated to buy from you. But you'd better not try this with strangers. They'll laugh you right out of the room."

Then there's recruiting. "You manage and motivate somebody?" snorts the self-image. "What gall you've got. Are you crazy? What gives you the right to tell anybody else how they ought to live their life? To tell them how to be successful? Let's look at your bank account. Who's kidding who? Look, let me protect you from certain humiliation and disappointment."

Some people, through sheer force of enthusiasm, and the pushing of the person who brought them into the business, may even go against the self-image's arguing, recruit a few people, and even have a bit of success. But that worried, skeptical self-image will be standing there, feet dug in, pulling backwards, trying as hard as it can to drag that person back to safety. And the first time a thing or two goes wrong—snap!—the self-image will pull you back.

Now here's my point, and it's a simple one: you cannot outperform your self-image for very long, and neither can distributors you bring into your organization. If you are to succeed in network marketing, you must go to work strengthening your self-image and rushing it into shape to meet the challenges of this particular activity. If you are to help the people you recruit achieve success, you've got to get them on a self-image strengthening program too.

What are the requirements of this job? You have to see yourself as the success you are becoming rather than as the person you've been in the past. You have to be able to communicate clearly and persuade confidently. You have to develop a leader's persona. We are talking about nothing less than a transformation in the way you think, talk, act, and invest your time.

A person who has the habit of pessimism, selling him- or herself and others short, joining with others in complaining about how unfair life is, and going home everyday, plopping down on the couch, and saying "I'm whipped" is going to need a total attitude and behavior makeover! He or she must learn, desire, and cultivate the habit of optimism, and must see talent within when no one else sees it, along with talent in others that even they do not see in themselves. He/she must focus on opportunity instead of inequity. And after a full day's work at the factory, office or store, this person must rush home, quickly re-energize, and begin coaching distributors by phone or get dressed and go to a meeting.

Let me mention another challenge. Actually I have mentioned it, but let me now highlight it. You need confidence and the courage of your convictions more in this business than in most. Here, you will be telling others what to do to be successful when, in reality, you may not yet have success of your own to back up your advice. You must borrow your unshakable conviction from others who are highly successful in your business.

Now that I have told you of these difficulties, let me assure you that the fundamentals of Psycho-Cybernetics can help you conquer them all!

You will become the successful distributor in the Theater of Your Mind before you become that success in real life, and that is how you will reprogram your self-image. Because success breeds success, and because synthetic success is just as powerful as actual success in affecting the self-image, you will find it very helpful to "ingest" as much success as you can. By that I mean, listening to the tapes recorded by people who are successful in your business, reading the books they have written, attending the seminars they present, and not just casually observing but seriously studying how they handle themselves and respond to others. Imprint what they do and how they do it into your own subconscious mind, then see yourself doing those same things that same way, in your own mental movies.

What about leadership? Are you a leader? There's an old saying that it is difficult to lead a cavalry charge if you think you look funny sitting on a horse. This is another way of pointing out that the self-image must be up to the task. It's my observation that just about everybody has leadership qualities waiting to be awakened. I'm sure that you do too.

I have a somewhat self-serving suggestion: Each time you recruit a new person into your organization, either give him or her the book *Psycho-Cybernetics* as a gift or encourage him/her to go to a bookstore, buy it and read it. Each time you get a person interested in the workings of the Automatic Success Mechanism, you significantly enhance the likelihood of his or her success. If you can get that person to read this book too, so much the better.

Beyond this, understand that, to a great degree, your leadership role in network marketing can be summarized as *installing belief*. It is your job to install belief in that new person's subconscious mind; belief in your products, opportunity, company, and leadership. Of course, you must have it to give it.

Let me introduce you to one of the most successful belief-installers I've ever encountered. Jason Boreyko is the president of a young, fast-growing network marketing company, New Vision International. This company has gone from zero to over a quarter of a billion dollars in sales in less than 3 years. It's now the third largest of 2,000 companies in its industry. A bottle of their liquid mineral tonic is sold every four seconds, 24 hours a day, 7 days a week. An amazing success story. But when you meet and talk with Jason, there's no mystery to this success. Jason has an abundance of belief in himself, his products, his company, and his industry. He has an abundance of belief to transfer to others. If you examine the sources of his confidence, you'll discover the following.

First, Jason was raised by very optimistic, encouraging parents. His father and mother were successful in network marketing.

Jason's mother preached the gospel of big dreams, and his father taught that, with integrity, vision, hard work and teamwork, anything was possible. Of course, not everybody has the benefit of such an upbringing. But if you cannot recall having heard these things from your parents, it's never too late to seek out other authority figures to say these things to you now. The library is full of biographies, autobiographies and how-to books by and about successful, inspiring people who will tell you these same things about yourself and about life. You can create a "success environment" for yourself, beginning today.

Second, Jason had his share of hard knocks and learned from them that he is an individual of strength. He did not take to network marketing like a duck to water. For a while, he turned his back on the whole thing and worked at different, unchallenging jobs. When he did return to network marketing, he struggled and failed as a distributor with four different companies. When he, his brother and his Dad all built hugely successful distributorships with one company, giving them a combined income of over $350,000 a month, they had the rug pulled out from underneath them; the company abruptly went bankrupt. Their income stopped in a heartbeat.

Instead of being paralyzed by "Oh poor me . . . why me?. . . it's not fair!" or by depression, or fear, Jason and his brother sat down, evaluated what had gone wrong, put forward their own ideas about how to build the ideal network marketing company, and set out to do just that with New Vision. My point here is that your past disappointments and failures should have value to you. You haven't died from them. You haven't curled up into a ball and stayed there. If you will think about it, you, too, are a person with strength and resiliency inside, waiting to be called on and used to achieve greatness with the right opportunity.

Third, Jason has a mission. His mother died of cancer at a relatively young age, and the country's best and most expensive doctors could only stand by impotently. Jason is convinced that cancer, and other diseases, can be prevented with natural substances, nutrition, minerals and diet. He is inspired to spread this message. His mother's untimely death motivates him every day. This "missionary zeal" lifts up the self-image and strengthens its immune system against discouragement or criticism.

Selling Prevention

People in prevention-type businesses, such as home security systems, fire safety systems, insurance or, for business, theft control services, safety products, asset protection, and so on, often talk about "The Other Guy Syndrome." This is what stops these sales-people in their tracks; individuals' profound belief that disasters only happen to "the other guy."

Some years ago, I had an opportunity to visit with a man making over $200,000 a year selling fire alarm systems to homeowners. At the time, he outperformed the second most successful salesperson in his company by a four-times margin. He admitted that his was a very difficult business, and that it was rare for a day to pass without his questioning the wisdom of staying in it versus finding an easier product to sell. As you might imagine, my curiosity was sparked by that. And my short conversation with him reveals everything you need to know about thriving in this kind of tough selling environment.

MM: So why don't you go find something easier to sell?

DENNIS: Dr. Maltz, as I told you, I think about it. I surely do. But there are three things that keep me in this business.

MM: One of them must be the money.

DENNIS: No, not really. Oh, I wouldn't work for free, but I've never really worried about the money either. The income is a by-product of those other three things. One is that I kind of relish being able to succeed where so many fail, to do something that's so difficult for just about everybody else to do. Two is that I honestly believe every home in America desperately needs what I sell. If you've ever seen a burn victim from a house fire, especially a kid, and of course, you have, then you have to get sick when you see a house full of kids, with no fire alarms. Or just a dime store smoke detector. So I feel like I'm doing something important. I tell people that I save lives for a living, but to me that's not some corny slogan. I mean it. Three, this type of selling forces me to use mental powers most people never tap at all, and I value that discipline.

MM: What do you mean by mental powers?

DENNIS: Well, exactly the sort of thing you teach. For example, I have to use very vivid words, to create very vivid mental pictures for my customers. You know, they have to see their house on fire, their possessions destroyed, their kids burnt and scarred before they can buy. So I have to get those pictures across. And I've learned that I have to have those images in my mind before I can convey them to others. It's all about using and activating the human imagination.

MM: What else?

DENNIS: I need to get into a certain state of mind. I call it 110% Convinced, 110% Determined, before each sales presentation. About six years ago, I made a presentation to one family I recall, and didn't close the sale. Three months later, I learned their house burned to the ground. The father and two kids got out alive. The mother didn't. And the little girl was very badly burned. When I heard about this, I had a nightmare about being confronted by that burnt, scarred little girl and having her yell at me: Why didn't you save my mommy, mister? I've used that nightmare ever since. I call that girl up in my mind right before every sales presentation. I sit there in my car and I can see her, just as clear and real as if she was right there with me, and I talk with her, and I promise her that I'm not going to let what happened to her happen to anybody else.

MM: What about this thing, "the other guy syndrome." How do you get past that?

DENNIS: You sure can't do it with logic. To tell you the truth,
           I don't know how to explain how I get past that in
           mechanical or technical terms. I see it as my con-
           viction coming up against their resistance. My
           conviction is almost always stronger than their
           resistance.

Selling Big Ticket Items

One man I know sells multiyear, comprehensive practice
management services to dentists. His average sale is $32,000. He
told me that the first time he had to get his lips around that number and ask a dentist to sign on the dotted line, he had to hold his
breath, afraid of what the doctor's reaction would be. He has gone
on to become one of the most relaxed, confident "big ticket" sales
professionals I've ever met, and he routinely earns over $250,000 a
year as a result.

Another woman I know, a financial planner and investment
broker who works for a developer of planned communities, sells
investments of $50,000 to $500,000. She told me that no one in her
family had ever accumulated $50,000 in their entire lives, let alone
put that princely sum into a single investment. She had to reprogram her self-image to do it. The last I heard from her, she had sold
an eight-million dollar project in a record five weeks.

Several of my co-authors sell very expensive consulting services, often asking a client for $15,000 to ten times that much, thou-
sands of dollars for just one day of advice-giving. Imagine asking
clients for $500, $700, $1,000 an hour? My colleagues do it without
blinking.

I've also known a number of salespeople who tried to step up
to big-ticket selling and choked. Why should the dollar amount of
the sale be a problem? Actually, there are many reasons. But they
all link to the state of the self-image.

There's guilt. Guilt at taking so much money from somebody.
Guilt at making such a big commission from a single sale, from a single day's work. Guilt because the salesperson is not so thoroughly

convinced of the value that the price is tiny by comparison, though big by most other standards.

There are preconceived beliefs about what other people can afford. Many salespeople know that paying their price may present a financial hardship to the customer, and cannot bring themselves to ask anybody to make such a sacrifice. Can you see how these are all self-image issues?

I know a chiropractor who gets over half of all of his new patients to prepay for months of care, prescribed as a "package." His average prepay case is $6,000. I said to him that $6,000 was a lot of money for most families.

"Yes," he said, "I suppose it is. But I know that when they make this kind of a financial commitment, they are much more likely to follow through on every single one of my recommendations, adhere to their treatment and self-care programs, and regain their health. And what can be more important than their health? So if they have to give up cable TV, movies, a vacation or take out a loan to make this commitment, that doesn't bother me one bit. I know that they and I are doing the right thing."

Let me add that I know a great many very fine chiropractors who would never dare sit across their desks from new patients and ask them to write out $6,000 checks. Some of them criticize this doctor. They do not like him "selling" his patients these treatment programs. They call it unprofessional. But I know the true reason they disapprove and do not do what he does, even though they'd love to have the result he has; a million dollar a year practice.

I don't know if I've hit on your particular "extra tough" selling situation in this chapter or not. I do know that just about any salesperson has within everything necessary to excel in any extra tough selling environment. Your self-image is incredibly flexible, generous and capable. Whatever you sincerely ask of it, you can become.

Chapter 4

How to Be Confident and Persuasive in Group Presentations and Public Speaking

You are the lucky one; you have been chosen to make your company's presentation to the group of key executives from ABC Corporation, the largest company of its kind. If your firm gets this account, its sales will almost double overnight. You might even make partner. There's just one small problem: the very thought of standing up in front of a group and speaking has your knees knocking, hands shaking, and stomach quaking. You can feel the blood draining out of your face at the very thought of public speaking. The last time you tried was at a civic club meeting. You stumbled over words, nervously lost your place several times and fumbled with your notes, sweat right through your shirt, and just wanted it all to be over so you could slink home and hide.

Having the ability to speak to 10 or 1,000 confidently and persuasively is of incredible value to many sales professionals because resistance disappears with you as the authority on the platform. Because public speaking remains the number-one fear, kings and queens, CEOs and celebrities, fear it and are in awe of anybody who does it. People have been conditioned to see the person in front of the room as an authority. You gain stature and power just by being there.

A friend of mine, a financial planner and investment counselor in New York, frequently speaks at Chamber of Commerce meetings, city or state association conventions of every group from doctors to plumbers, and other, similar venues. He tells me that his best clients come to him as a result of these speeches. From these people, there is no fee resistance, no resistance to his recommendations. Clients turn portfolios of $100,000 to several million over to him like compliant little puppy dogs. Why does he get to acquire clients like this, with zero resistance?

He *positions* himself; doesn't go prospecting. His speaking has given him such stature in these clients' eyes there's no reason to question him.

Now, truth be told, the fact that someone has the ability to get up in front of a group and dispense information in an interesting way is not necessarily a guarantee he or she has great expertise in financial planning. But a great many well-to-do people are impressed by these presentations and do make that leap-of-faith connection. It is for this reason alone that smart sales professionals invest the time and energy to become good at public speaking.

How to Switch Your Focus and Banish Fear

Most people feel fearful about speaking in front of a group. When I ask people what frightens them most about public speaking, most reply that they fear making a fool of themselves, or somehow humiliating and embarrassing themselves. Well, we have all embarrassed ourselves at one time or another. Who will forget President George Bush vomiting at the dinner in China, and having it seen on TV by millions? Has there been a U.S. President who has not made a serious, embarrassing mistake in one of his speeches? It happens to the best of us. Still, you do not want to suffer an embarrassing or humiliating experience, and the fear of that happening can be paralyzing.

One solution that has worked for me as well as others I have coached is to switch the focus from *me* to *them*. When you focus on yourself, you may very well raise your anxiety level. You ask yourself: Will I make some dumb mistake? Will I forget something? Will I stammer? Will I . . . this or that? You are cranking up the intensity of the spotlight on you to an intolerable level. And quite frankly, you are being a bit selfish and self-centered.

Instead, try focusing on the audience. I think about who these people are, what their needs are, what their daily experiences are like, and what they may be hoping to hear or learn and take home as a result of being there. I also use mental pictures like this one: thick, colorful threads of communication, persuasion, inspiration and motivation come out of my heart and plug into the hearts of the audience members, threads of strong connection between me and them. I see our hearts and spirits perfectly connected.

Another good mental picture is that of the audience warming up. If you look out and see that the group waiting for you seems a bit cold, stiff, and uninviting, form a picture of them all frozen together in a big, thick block of ice. See warmth and energy emanating from you as you step up to the podium. The warm glow quickly melts the ice and frees the audience from their prison of discomfort, so they can enjoy the moment, stimulated by your ideas. As long as I hold onto images like these, images of anxiety cannot occur.

Keep this in mind, too: your audience wants you to succeed! Nobody wants to sit through a bad speech or suffer along with a failing speaker. Quite the opposite; the audience wants a good, interesting, enjoyable experience. Your audience is on your side.

If you are speaking to sell, keep in mind that your prospects want to buy! They're hoping you are going to present good solutions to their problems, viable ways of achieving their ambitions, and that you will be able to make them feel confident enough to take positive action on your good ideas. They're rooting for you!

Finally, keep in mind that most audiences, even critical, skeptical, analytical audiences, are generous and forgiving of minor stumbles or bumbles. They are far less interested in your style than your message. If you have real value to deliver, people focus on that. They are not sitting there harshly judging each word, each gesture, with microscopic intensity.

How to Develop Your Platform Personality

Many people live unhappily by going through life wishing they could be someone else instead of working on the development of their own, unique personality. Don't make this mistake in life and don't make this mistake on the platform.

When I first started speaking about Psycho-Cybernetics, I experimented with mimicking the styles of other speakers. I tried telling jokes, and found those that got laughs for others flopped for me. I quickly decided that my platform personality should be me, not somebody else or a composite of others. So I started talking to my audiences from my heart, sharing my own life experiences. Not only did it get easier and easier for me to speak, but the response from the audiences got better and better.

I will cheerfully tell you, I never became the greatest speaker in the world. Dr. Norman Vincent Peale, for example, ran rings around me. But I did become the greatest speaker Maxwell Maltz was capable of being, each time I spoke.

One of the greatest attributes you can bring to your speeches, seminars, group sales presentations or Sunday School classes is *authenticity.* In a world increasingly filled with "plastic," people instinctively respond favorably to the person who presents him- or herself honestly, warts and all.

Will I Ever Get Over Stage Fright?

Some people perform their entire lives fighting stage fright before every performance. Barbra Streisand and Johnny Carson are two great examples. Even though Barbra can sell out every seat in virtually any theater any time she wishes to do so, Streisand stopped giving live concerts for many years because of stage fright. And when she does perform, she must battle this resistance every time. Even after years of doing "The Tonight Show," Johnny Carson admitted feeling a surge of fear immediately before stepping out through the curtain to face the audience.

Having *some* nervousness is actually useful, however. It means that you are taking the presentation seriously and can provide a surge of energy. Too much, of course, can paralyze you and severely impair your performance.

The truth is that you cause your own stage fright. There is no such thing as stage fright. In fact, we are born with only two fears, of loud noises and falling. Babies react with fear to the feeling of falling and to exceptionally loud, unfamiliar noises. However, babies have no other in-born fears. Fears we adults do battle with daily, like fear of rejection, embarrassment, street crime, and failure are all learned and acquired fears. We require certain life experiences to develop these fears. All such fears are internal, emotional responses to circumstances, real or imagined, because your Servo-Mechanism cannot tell the difference between real or vividly imagined experience. You have to either confront something that produces a feeling of fear, say a mugger in the street, a fire in your home, or a huge bear in the woods, or you must create something frightening in your imagination before you can have fright.

Obviously, some fear serves a very useful purpose. Feeling fear tells you that your Servo-Mechanism is working on your request. But when fears paralyze, they are unhealthy, and require treatment.

Here are some of the ways you might whip yourself into a frightened, paralyzed state of mind, and how to conquer this:

1. Making unfair demands on yourself. If you approach a speech with the idea that you must "wow" the group as they have never before been "wowed," have them rolling in the aisles with laughter one minute, crying the next, and giving you a standing ovation the next, you set the bar of success so high even the top pros in speaking might fall short. Relax, my friend, and be a bit more realistic. The situation you are in probably does not require the greatest performance ever given by a speaker. Focus on the practical results you desire. Do not compare yourself to other speakers either. Be your best self.

When people have come to me for counseling, I'm often astounded at how severely and harshly they judge themselves. You must see yourself with kind eyes! You must give yourself the gift of compassion!

2. Having unfair expectations of others. I talked with a young chiropractor after he had given a speech to a local club. He was terribly disappointed that only two of the forty people there had sought him out afterwards, to schedule appointments at his clinic. He was kicking himself black-and-blue for a myriad of real and imagined faults in his speech and blaming himself for squandering a great opportunity to flood his office with new patients.

I told him he expected too much of himself, of one event, and certainly of his audience. Those forty people brought with them all sorts of distractions. Some were never really paying attention and he might not have gotten their attention even if he set something on fire. Others vehemently distrust chiropractic philosophy and are not going to be persuaded. They listened with locked-shut minds. Or, some probably have doctors they're happy with, and so on. In other words, all forty of those people could not reasonably be expected to respond. In fact, only a few of them could be expected to.

I asked him: if you mail out forty letters to people in a club you belong to or neighborhood you live in, inviting them in for an examination, how many will respond? At best one, but it's closer to one out of one hundred. I also asked him what a typical patient was worth in dollars to the practice. His answer was $800. So, two new patients from an hour's speech, $1,600. Not bad. I pointed out that he had gotten plenty of applause, and people asked questions, so the door was wide open to continue to communicate with those thirty-eight people, to get some of them into his clinic over time. He had "broken the ice" with those thirty-eight people. They now knew him, had a face put with his name, and probably had a favorable opinion of him. And he had immediately secured two new patients without incurring even a cent of advertising expense.

"When you look at it that way," he said, "I did pretty well, didn't I?" Yes he did. I thought he had accomplished a lot with just one brief speech, and I told him so.

3. *"Mistakeaphobia."* Are you desperately afraid of making a mistake? There's a famous story about an actor in a Broadway play, a serious murder mystery. On opening night, at the appointed moment, he picked the prop gun up off the table, aimed and fired at the other actor he was to kill. The gun didn't fire. He pulled the trigger. Click. No bang. Again. Click. No bang. "Damn," he said, tossing the useless gun aside, "then I shall use Plan B and kill you with my poison-tipped shoe." With that, he kicked the surprised actor in his back-end, sending him sprawling, and he strode off the stage.

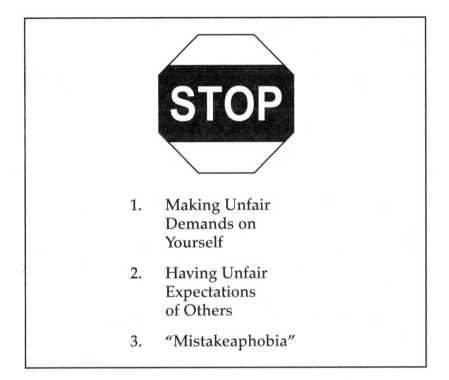

1. Making Unfair Demands on Yourself

2. Having Unfair Expectations of Others

3. "Mistakeaphobia"

The reviews in the papers the next day all praised him mightily for his quick thinking, unflappability, and good humor. (His fellow actor was not so generous with his praise!)

My point is that mistakes happen. Yes, you may forget some part of your speech. Yes, you may mispronounce a word. The lights may go out. The microphone fail. Your slides may show up on the screen upside down. We are all mistake makers, because perfection was never bestowed on humanity. But we are all also mistake breakers, capable of rising above our mistakes with the right combination of humility and pride, determination and good humor. Always remind yourself: "Yes, I am a Mistake Maker, but I am also a great Mistake Breaker."

You might also remember that your audience doesn't have your notes. They aren't checking you, to catch a mistake. Remember the Ross Perot TV infomercials of the 1992 Presidential elections? What if I told you that he accidentally left out two graphs and skipped over an entire"chunk"of his presentation? Did you notice it then? Am I telling you the truth—did he or didn't he? What difference does it make?

Face the fact that the gun isn't always going to go bang. A mistake or two are going to happen. Just move forward as best you can. In order to succeed, we must be willing to make mistakes and have them noticed sometimes. We must risk to move ahead.

Never Let 'Em See You Sweat

That became a popular line in commercials for a deodorant product. It's a good slogan for speakers, because the worst thing you can do with an audience is show or tell them that you are not in control. For example, the worst opening line ever invented is: "Unaccustomed as I am to public speaking. . . ." This tells the audience: *Look out! I'm going to be awful. Boring. Stumbling all over myself.* This tells the audience: *Look for the mistakes! Be critical!*

Never apologize to an audience, in advance or later. Do your very best job. Press on. Even while you may feel you are suffering and struggling, most of the audience will be tuned in to your message, impressed that you have the courage to be up there in the first place, and oblivious to the little difficulties that you are having and that feel so big to you.

I once followed a young minister on a day-long program at a very large church in southern California. There were over 1,000 people in attendance and, before going on, the young minister told me he'd never addressed more than 100 people before in his life. I watched him deliver his speech, and, while he made a little slip here or there, and was obviously a bit nervous, I thought he did well and, more importantly, the audience responded to him very enthusiastically. He left the stage to thunderous applause. During the brief break between his presentation and mine, I went over and congratulated him.

"Dr. Maltz, thank you but congratulations definitely are *not* in order," he said, "I was terrible!"

"Terrible?" I said incredulously. "But the audience loved you and your message. Didn't you hear their laughter, see their nods of agreement, and hear their applause?"

"Yes," the minister said, "but I left out an entire part of my material. I had five points and skipped the third one! And my hands were shaking. I must have looked like a scared schoolboy up there."

I told him that none of that mattered much. That he should be proud of having done his best and of having connected so well with the audience. Unfortunately, he would hear none of it and went home disappointed and frustrated with himself. He magnified his mistakes and minimized his success, even though the audience did just the opposite. What a terrible thing to do to yourself! Why be your own hanging judge when the jury wants to acquit?

You see, no one in that young minister's audience leaped up and yelled, "Hey, you forgot your point number three!" And even if they had, so what? He might as well have relaxed and enjoyed the success that he had, instead of putting himself on the burner and turning up the flame. Don't make his mistake. Don't cook yourself in your own juices of fear, insecurity and harsh self-criticism. See yourself and your performance with kind eyes. Magnify what you do well and minimize your mistakes.

He should have told his Critic Within to shut up, sit in the corner and look at the reactions of the thousand people in the audience. You've probably noticed that some of the most loudly criticized movies, by the critics, have been the biggest hits at the box office, loved by the public. Your Critic Within can be helpful in giving you feedback for improvement, but if the critic gets too big for your good, you must remind this naysayer that he or she is unjustifiably harsher in judgment than the people whose votes really count; your audience, customers, clients.

Once I arrived at a speaking engagement, minutes away from addressing a group of fifty or sixty corporate executives and CEOs. When I opened up my briefcase, my notes were missing. Frantically, I sorted through everything in the attaché case, searched my suitcoat pockets, to no avail "Calm down Max," I told myself. "Relax. After all, you know your material. You wrote a whole book about it. You've given speeches, even long seminars about this. You don't need your notes." Then I thought, maybe I just need a slightly different game plan. After a few minutes' thought, a little quiet relaxation and mental rehearsal, I went out and told the group that I didn't want to just lecture to them from the same notes I used for every group; I wanted to talk about their most pressing concerns. I asked them for their biggest frustrations in dealing with others, motivating employees and their nagging personal concerns, and I listed them on a white pad on an easel. Then I talked about how Psycho-Cybernetics related to those things. We had a lively, provocative two hour conversation, and the time was used up before any of us realized. And they never saw me sweat!

Afterward, I could have beat myself up mentally for being so dumb as to forget my notes like some disorganized fool or rank amateur. Instead, I was able to congratulate myself for rising to the occasion and celebrate discovering a new and different way to deliver my message. I had truly been a Mistake Maker but also, more importantly, a Mistake Breaker.

Get Into a Winning State

There is no longer any question that certain kinds of mental preparation can ensure improved performance. The currently popular term is *state*. It means the mental, emotional and physiological condition you are in at the moment. In sports, it is sometimes called *the zone*. There are people who can get into a certain state that allows them to break thick wooden boards with their hands or head or walk across hot coals or lay flat on a bed of nails without the slightest injury. These are demonstrations of the awesome powers of the mind to control physical reality.

Try this: think back to a particularly stressful time from the past week. Maybe right after a presentation went wrong or a chewing-out from the sales manager. Maybe your anxiety level was high, between presentations. Or your frustration level was high. Put yourself back into that time. Feel the tension, just as you did at that moment.

Now imagine walking from there right out to a podium, in front of a group of important people, to deliver a speech. How effective would you be under those conditions? Not very. You'd be distracted. Unable to focus and concentrate. Uptight.

Now try this: think back to a time this past week when everything was going well. Maybe right after closing a big sale. Feel that joy, enthusiasm, and surge of confidence. Imagine going from there right to the podium, to deliver a speech. How effective would you be under those conditions? Probably pretty good. Confidence breeds confidence. You'd have a high level of energy. You'd be loose and relaxed.

The situation is the same in both scenarios. But your state of mind, your state of energy, your state of confidence, is very different in the two scenarios. And the outcome would undoubtedly be significantly different.

Most pro speakers have mental conditioning regimens they run through immediately before speaking, to get into the most focused, dynamic, confident state possible. Some do relaxation exercises, if they have anxieties about speaking to groups. Others have exercises to bring their energy levels up. Some go into the Theater of Your Mind and run a mental movie of their best speaking experience. One way or another, the pro speaker gets into a preferred state.

As you do more and more speaking, you can experiment and find the prespeech regimen that works for you. One of the top Tupperware salespeople in the country told me that she had terrible fears and anxieties about conducting the home parties and giving the group presentations when she first started out. Her experience was that, even though she felt nervous, unfocused and was making mistakes, the customers didn't seem to notice, had a good time and bought. Soon she was using that in her warm-up exercise. She would find a quiet place, usually the bathroom, look herself in the mirror and say: "Helen, you always do well. You may make mistakes or be nervous, but the groups always have a good time and buy a lot of product anyway, so you should relax and have a good time too." Then she would rerun a mental movie of a successful party. Finally, she bounced up and down on her toes for a minute or two and called up an unlimited supply of positive, dynamic energy. When she went out into the living room to start the party, she was "in state."

Whether you speak 10 times a year or 100 times a year, this strategy can work for you too.

Secrets of a Compelling, Convincing Presentation

The good news is that many of the components of a compelling, convincing group presentation or speech, to 10 or 10,000, are exactly the same as the ones you already understand and use in your one-on-one sales presentations. In other words, selling is selling. For example, you undoubtedly use client or customer testimonials, expert endorsements, competitive comparisons, and statistics in your one-on-one presentations. You'll probably want to use those same things in your presentation to a group.

In addition to transferring what works for you one-on-one to the stage, here are a few top pros' key secrets for maximizing the impact of your speech.

Customize to Connect

Most top sales pros turn their noses up at canned, scripted presentations. They know that delivering the same presentation to different prospects gets very poor results. Each audience deserves a different presentation, too. The more you know about the group you are going to speak to, the better, so you can customize your remarks. To connect with an audience, customize your speech for that audience. Learn what is going on in their industry or community and target your speech to those timely concerns. Learn the jargon of the group, so you can use a little of it.

On the other hand, do not pretend to be an insider when you are not. This is just another way of trying to appear as someone other than yourself. If you are to succeed on the platform, you must be you. But you can show the audience that you thought enough of them and took your opportunity seriously enough to learn something about them, their business, experiences, and terminology.

Organize to Open Minds

I'm always dismayed when a speaker rambles on and on, and wanders around like a poor soul lost in the woods. This speaker has no hope of connecting with his or her audience, and isn't even connected with him- or herself! Do you know what people do when they are confronted with confusing, hard to decipher information? They close their minds. You may want to accuse them of intellectual laziness and you might even be right. But that won't help you sell. It is very important to deliver your presentation in an organized, easy to follow manner.

I often used acronyms in my speeches, like SUCCESS, 'S' for Sense Of Direction, 'U' for Understanding, 'C' for Courage, 'C' for Charity or Compassion, 'E' for Esteem, 'S' for Self-Confidence and 'S' for Self-Acceptance. Some people say that using such acronyms is corny, and that may be, but I always found them helpful in organizing my thoughts and helping the audience stay with me. Whether you use acronyms, numbering, like "10 secrets of. . . ," or a classic, much-taught formula for a speech, like "Tell them what you are going to tell them, tell them, and tell them what you told them," or all these methods, your goal should be to prepare and deliver such a well-organized presentation that every person in the room can stay with you easily.

To succeed, you must accept 100% of the responsibility for succeeding. So, if you seek success on the platform, as a persuasive speaker, you must accept 100% of the responsibility for putting your message across. You cannot reasonably expect the audience to work hard at getting your message. They work on their jobs. They certainly don't need to work hard doing yours too!

Be Personal to Persuade

I think you have to get personal in order to persuade. You have to open up to others to get them to open up to you. If you are passionate about your product or proposition because of your personal experiences, don't keep that secret; reveal yourself and share your honest emotions. If something humorous or mildly embarrassing has happened to you, that illustrates an important point. Share your embarrassing moment; it makes it easier for the audience to connect with you.

My recommendation to beginning speakers is not to use jokes. Telling jokes well is much more difficult than it appears to be, and laying an egg can throw you off for the rest of your presentation. Instead of others' jokes, use your own personal, true stories.

I have many favorite stories I've used in many of my lectures, which have also found their way into my books. For instance, a story about being trapped in the hallway of my high-rise apartment building during a power black-out. Of meeting one of the happiest people on earth, on an exotic tropical island. The story of being sold my Burberry topcoat. Many of these stories reveal my own humanity, human frailties, even my own arguments with myself, in my efforts to be the big Max versus the small Max, to activate my Success Mechanism rather than my Failure Mechanism. These stories are not always totally flattering, but they are true, and illustrate my points.

S U C C E S S

S   ense of direction

U   nderstanding

C   ourage

C   ompassion

E   steem

S   elf-confidence

S   elf-acceptance

By the way, the telling of interesting stories is, in itself, a very powerful selling strategy. People naturally, automatically perk up when a story is told. Why? Because they have been programmed to! As children, we learn to like having stories read to use at bedtime or as a treat. Scouts have fun telling stories around the campfire. As we grow a little older, we enjoy hearing the "grown-ups" tell stories of the most important events and experiences in their lives. The salesperson or speaker who learns to illustrate important points with good stories has a big advantage.

Use Pictures to Penetrate

Nothing penetrates resistance like a dynamic picture. We think in pictures. We are controlled by a self-image. We all know the phrases "a picture is worth a thousand words" and "seeing is believing." Pictures, horrible pictures, sold the American public on demanding the Vietnam War be ended. Pictures, terrible pictures, of poorly fed, emaciated, mistreated children inspire us to donate millions of dollars to organizations that feed, clothe, medicate and educate the deprived children of the world. Pictures of exotic, beautiful, romantic beaches and oceans make Hawaii the "dream vacation" of thousands of people, who then scrimp and save and budget and plan for years for the "trip of a lifetime." The picture of Michael Dukakis, clumsily perched on a tank, did much to nip his Presidential campaign in the bud. Pictures of beautiful people sell millions of dollars of perfumes, cosmetics and clothing. Evidence abounds demonstrating the power of pictures.

When the great artist Salvador Dali wanted to express his feelings about Psycho-Cybernetics, and to thank me for my influence on his life, he painted a magnificent picture: a figure of a man, coming out of the dark shadows into the bright sunlight, sharing this space with a sailboat being guided toward a destination. He summarized my books and lectures in a single, powerful painting. I admire his talent. And I was again awestruck at the way a single picture can do the work of thousands of words.

My message is obvious: use pictures! Slides, overhead transparencies, easily understood charts or graphs all help you connect with your audience. You do not want to overdo this, and become secondary to high-tech gizmos. But you definitely *do* want to combine your words with pictures for maximum impact.

Ask for Action

Here's a very important secret of top sales pros who get great results from giving group presentations, speeches and seminars: they always ask for specific action from their audiences.

You must have a definite goal for your speech or presentation. You must see your audience of ten or ten thousand responding exactly as you ask them to, so that your goal is achieved!

I have watched any number of salespeople and speakers "wimp out" when it comes time to wrap up and ask the audience to act. This is where your self-image must step up to the plate for you. Your strong, confident self-image, your pride in what you represent, and your sense of purpose and direction must come together, to support you. You cannot get what you do not clearly and directly ask for.

One of the most powerful speakers that I've ever seen would usually begin wrapping up his presentation with the words: "Now, here is what we are going to do. . . ." He would then tell the audience exactly what he wanted them to do; complete a simple form being passed out by his assistants, go to a display outside the meeting room, line up, and turn in the forms to purchase his products. He spelled it out in exact detail. Without flinching. And often 80% to 90% of all the people in the audience happily and eagerly followed his instructions and did exactly as asked. Although this particular speaker did this with more *certainty* than other speakers I've seen, a number of top pro speakers follow this same model, including the co-authors of this book. What these top professional speakers do to typically create revenues of a million dollars a year or more, you can do to get the action you desire from your audiences.

As you can see, it is in your absolute best interest to have clarity of purpose and the courage to ask for precisely the result you desire.

Power of Association

Association is one of the most powerful forces governing the outcomes of humans' lives, third only to the programming of the self-image and habit. If a person's best friends at work are all avid golfers, it is a fairly safe wager that he or she will become interested in golf. If the novice golfer plays with better golfers, it is a fairly safe wager that he/she will improve in playing the game.

SECRETS OF COMPELLING PRESENTATIONS

1. CUSTOMIZE to Connect

2. ORGANIZE to Open Minds

3. Be PERSONAL to Persuade

4. Use PICTURES to Penetrate

We recognize the importance of *negative* association in many different ways. Parents worry, justifiably, about their sons or daughters falling in with "the wrong crowd." When convicts are released from prison on parole or probation, one of the most common rules imposed restricts them from fraternizing with known felons or frequenting bars and pool halls populated by other criminals, because it is known that such fraternization greatly increases the likelihood of that person committing another crime and returning to prison. Oddly, many people know this but do not look for opportunities to use it to their advantage, through *positive* association.

The principle is simple: if you aspire to the highest possible income in selling, seek out and associate with top money earners in selling. If you are eager to improve as a public speaker, the two best favors you can do for yourself are 1) to associate with other people working on improving their speaking skills and, 2) put yourself into situations where you get practice and experience speaking.

If you are just beginning to perfect your confidence and skill as a speaker, consider taking the Dale Carnegie Course or joining a Toastmasters International group in your area. You can find both of these organizations in your local telephone directories.

If you aspire to speaking professionally, contact the National Speakers Association in Phoenix, Arizona, for information about membership, seminars, and a chapter in your area. By the way, you *can* become a professional speaker and gain worldwide recognition if that is your goal. Zig Ziglar, arguably today's most famous and beloved motivational speaker, began his movement in that direction as a salesman, selling pots and pans door-to-door. Tom Hopkins, arguably America's best-known sales trainer, began as a real estate salesman. Everyone of this book's co-authors began as a sales professional and transitioned to professional speaking without benefit of any formal training. These speakers: Mr. Ziglar, Mr. Hopkins, my co-authors, all speak to tens of thousands to hundreds of thousands of people each year. They were not born with any gene left out of their biology. They were not given any education you cannot readily obtain.

Chapter 5

How to Zoom Out of a Selling Slump

Nothing's more troubling and frustrating than a genuine slump." You believe you are doing exactly the same things that have been successful for you, yet success now eludes you at every turn. You dig in, grit your teeth, stiffen your back and try even harder, but still you cannot get back on track. Impenetrable resistance surrounds you like a steel cage. You begin to question your knowledge, doubt your competence, wonder if you've lost it. You feel that people are whispering behind your back, noting that you've slipped, fallen and can't get up! Your self-image is rapidly shrinking to the size of a small potato. Anxiety born of desperation occurs before every sales call. How will you break free of such a downward spiral?

I have known pro athletes who get into slumps, who try the most amazing things to break free, such as wearing their underwear backwards, shaving their heads, refusing to eat or have sex until they get out of the slump. Incredible!

The truth is no one can sustain peak performance day in and day out, for every game, presentation, or situation. Everybody has down days, where everything seems out of whack. Top performers in every field experience this, and shrug it off. The great quarterback Warren Moon was having an off night, unfortunately telecast worldwide on Monday Night Football. He fumbled twice, threw three interceptions, and generally looked like a rookie. Late in the game, standing helplessly on the sidelines while the opposing team turned yet another of his sloppy fumbles into a march down field for a touchdown, Warren had the deer-caught-in-the-glare-of-the-headlights look. One of the announcers commented, "This is a night Warren will want to forget." The other announcer, an explayer, said simply "And he will." He'd better! (All "money players" have short memories for mistakes, and great confidence in themselves.)

Yes, everybody has their slumps. Every business has troubled times, every marriage its periods of difficulty or distance, and every individual has moodiness. The problem is not really the slump; it is how we respond to it.

The Salesman Who Desperately Needed Surgery, But Not in His Nose

When I was still in private surgical practice, a young salesman came to consult with me about having an operation on his nose. When I asked what he did for a living, he said "I'm in sales, but I'm quitting."

His nose was slightly larger than normal or average, but certainly not as repulsive as he insisted, so I knew there was something interesting going on inside this fellow's self-image. He described his nose as big and fat and bulbous, like a cartoon character's. He believed that prospects were secretly laughing at him behind his back because of his nose.

When I pressed him for his story, I got the facts. It was a fact that three customers had called his manager recently, each complaining about his rude and hostile behavior. It was a fact that he hadn't made a sale in three weeks. And it was a fact that his boss had put him on notice: get with it or get gone.

"I'm not going to give him the satisfaction of canning me," he said. "I'm going to quit. Then I want you to fix this damned nose of mine, so I can go and get a better job."

I suggested that we delay the surgery for 30 days while he tried some facial stretching exercises that might make his nose slightly smaller and thinner, which, quite honestly, were the equivalent of a placebo; a sugar pill; because there are no exercises that can actually do that. But I took him through several facial movements and prescribed twenty repetitions of each one, everyday. Then I also suggested that he delay quitting his job for that same month.

"You can always quit," I told him, "but if that's what you want to do, and you want to change occupations, why not go out a winner instead of a loser? Exit with your head held high. Leave to move on to better things, not to escape failure. If we can find a way for you to make a number of sales, you could leave with a fat commission check to tide you over, and something to brag about on your resume."

I knew he needed *emotional* surgery. He was blaming his nose for his selling problems, but that just could not be the case. It was his hostility that was the problem. He had a chip on his shoulder and his prospects sensed it, didn't like it and got rid of him as quickly as they could.

I had him tell me of some of his early successes in his sales job. This fellow had once been on the fast track, opening new accounts and securing important new clients at a record-breaking pace. But his early success had stalled, and he seemed unable to get back in gear.

His slump started right after his girlfriend broke up with him and started dating another man he viewed as more handsome than he was. So here was my prescription:

First, every morning, while he did the facial exercises I had prescribed, he was to go into the Theater of Your Mind and replay mental movies of his most successful selling experiences. Second, he was to drop in on a past, happy customer he had a good relationship with first thing each day, with a half dozen doughnuts for the staff, a flower for the receptionist, just because "I was in the neighborhood and wanted to thank you for the past business." I hoped this would get him in a positive frame of mind. He would never think of these people as laughing at him or being repulsed by him; they did business with him and welcomed him cheerfully. Third, after each sales call during the day, win, lose or draw, he was to take a few minutes in his car to defuse his frustration and relax, and I gave him a little relaxation exercise to do. Fourth, I told him to go to sleep each night picturing his nose shrinking, until it was the perfect size and shape.

Finally, I said, "I want you to take some time and reason with yourself when you miss a sale or at the end of the day. Forget temporarily that the prospect may have noticed your oversize nose. You are an intelligent, mature adult and so is he or she; you are not children in the school yard. Think of all the important matters your prospect must be thinking about. Do you really think he or she has time to dwell on the look of your nose? Really listen to questions and objections and consider them at face value. Is there legitimacy there? Is there a clue as to how you might strengthen your presentation? Give your prospect the benefit of the doubt, assume he or she is sincere, pretend your nose has nothing to do with it, and look for ways you might sell your proposition more effectively. Even if you are right about your nose being a handicap in selling, if you want to go out a winner, you must rise above it. You must sell so persuasively you cannot be resisted, much like someone with a really severe physical handicap, like a severed spinal cord and wheelchair confinement, must rise above the physical pain and inconvenience and the emotional trauma in order to still be a good parent and a productive member of society. Like Roosevelt, who could, at times, barely rise up out of his wheelchair was still able to inspire an entire nation to rise up out of despair." I wrote all that down for him on a piece of paper and suggested he read it after a frustrating selling experience. I also gave him a copy of *Psycho-Cybernetics* and sent him on his way.

About two months later, I got a telephone call from the sales manager at the company where this young man worked. The salesman's turnaround had been so profound, the sales manager kept after him, to find out how he had changed his results, and, obviously, his personality so dramatically, so quickly, and the young man had told him about his meeting with me and my book. "I want to buy 100 copies of that book and get them over here as quickly as possible," the sales manager said.

Can you see that this young man's slump existed first and foremost within his own self-image? The real world results were just a mirror-like reflection of the turmoil and unhappiness in control of his self-image. All I did was interrupt his piling on of erroneous and harmful beliefs about how others saw him. I gave his self-image a breather from the constant destructive input, so it could break free and demonstrate to him that all was not dark and dismal.

If you find yourself in a slump, you must begin the exit by giving your self-image a break. Let it up off the mat. Don't keep slamming it to the ground, repeatedly piling the same input about what is wrong with the world, your life, your customers, your company and yourself on top of it.

How to Give Your Self-Image a Break and Zoom Out of a Slump

Let's review the steps I put this young salesman through, as practical actions you can do:

1. Recall and relive past successes. When a salesperson gets into a slump, he or she begins to question his/her abilities. Maybe I've lost my touch. Maybe I don't know what I'm doing, and so on. By reliving past successes, you *disprove* these failure-oriented ideas. You reaffirm your worth, competence, and knowledge. Go into the Theater of Your Mind and build some vivid, detailed mental movies of your most successful, exciting selling experiences. Spend a little time each morning relaxed, eyes closed, running these movies. Keep a little notepad handy to jot down the principles, ideas, and techniques you notice that you used in order to complete those sales, as if you were preparing to teach your methods to other salespeople.

2. Do something certain to reinforce a successful self-image. Arrange the first phone call or meeting of each day with a past or present satisfied, happy customer. When a coach is trying to give a young quarterback confidence after the quarterback has done poorly, he/she has the quarterback throw a couple "high probability" passes, to re-engage the feeling of being successful. You are your coach. Start each day by putting yourself in a high-probability situation, where only good things are likely to occur.

3. Relax. Do not go into a presentation or head for the next one if you feel angry, frustrated, or "tight." Allow a little time to debrief yourself and to relax between appointments. If you need specific relaxation exercises, you can find them in my first book *Psycho-Cybernetics.*

4. Reason with yourself. Think! You are an intelligent adult, capable of sorting out reality from fantasy, logic from emotion. Are you jinxed or hexed? There's no such thing. On Friday the 13th, someone will hit the lottery, someone will land a huge contract, someone will catch an early flight and be home in time to see her son's Little League game. Also on Friday the 13th, someone will lose a fortune in a bad business deal, someone will lose a key account, someone will miss the last flight of the day. These events have nothing whatsoever to do with it being Friday the 13th. There is no such thing as Friday the 13th hexes, jinxes, or even bad luck. If a prospect has refused to buy from you, it has nothing to do with your nose, whether the moon is full or not, or whether or not your lucky rabbit's-foot key chain is in your right or left pocket. Take responsibility, creatively question why the prospect made the decision, and find a way to use that information to make your next presentation better.

How to Give Your Self-Image a Break

1. Recall and relive past successes

2. Do something certain to reinforce a successful self-image

3. Relax

4. Reason with yourself

5. Take action

6. Inspire and motivate yourself

7. Program your Servo-Mechanism before going to sleep, to prepare for success the next day

5. *Take action.* One thing is certain: a ballplayer can't break out of a slump sitting on the bench, cowering in the dugout. You cannot break free of a slump hiding out at home or in the office, shuffling paper, pretending to be busy. Stop and reflect, take a bit of time to create a new plan of action, but then get on with it. Athletes will tell you, all superstitious goofiness aside, that they have to play their way out of a slump. You must do so too.

6. *Inspire and motivate yourself.* Rise above your frustration rather than give into it. Remember that all motivation is really self-motivation. Certainly attending a great seminar can help clear your head and renew your spirit; the Peter Lowe International "Success" Events that tour through dozens of cities each year are excellent for this purpose.* Certainly listening to an uplifting message on a cassette tape in your car can stimulate the imagination. But these are temporary, not lasting. You must develop the ability to motivate yourself, to be your own counselor, coach, booster and disciplinarian.

Waiting to somehow be inspired is waiting forever. Don't wait for inspiration to happen magically! As an author, I'm often asked how I have created so many books, articles, and other materials. Many other writers are often asked the same question. And there is a popular myth about writers that we lay around waiting for inspiration to strike, then leap to the typewriter, fingers flying over the keys. I sometimes wish this were true. Instead, most writers inspire and discipline themselves to write something every single day. The popular songwriter and novelist Jimmy Buffet says he never lets a morning pass without sitting down and writing at least a page of something. Me too.

I always cringed when I was introduced as a motivational speaker. I never wanted to be known as that, because I wanted to have more impact than a snack of Chinese food that leaves you hungry an hour later. You have a job to do, my friend, and that is to *motivate yourself.* Learning how to "flip your own switch" is what Psycho-Cybernetics is all about. While the world sits around waiting for someone or something to motivate it, you can rise to the very top of your profession by doing just the opposite.

(*Call 1-800-989-8990 for a schedule of cities and dates.)

How do you inspire yourself? How can you motivate yourself to action? How can you create energy, enthusiasm and optimism as needed, on demand? With exciting, vividly imagined, meaningful, worthwhile goals. With a strong, healthy self-image. With the simple understanding that all champions experience occasional slumps and that all champions rise above them, not by waiting for them to pass, but by working through them.

The truth is, if you find yourself in a slump, it's a pretty good bet that you put yourself there! But that's good news, not bad, because whatever we do we can change. If you are a Slump-Maker, then you are also a Slump-Breaker.

7. *Program your Servo-Mechanism each night before going to sleep, to prepare for success the next day*. Remember, your awesomely powerful Servo-Mechanism need *never* rest, and, solely dependent on your self-image's directives, is either a Success Mechanism or a Failure Mechanism. Before going to sleep at night, feel free to give it an assignment or two to work on, a quickly recalled vision of your near-term goals being achieved, a message of positive expectation for tomorrow. This will inspire your Success Mechanism to line up the resources, thoughts, ideas, know-how and confidence you need. It will magnetize you, to attract the cooperation you need from others. When you awake in the morning, on time, of your own accord, without requiring the prodding of an alarm clock, you will be full of optimism and energy.

Five Days to Breaking Free of Your Sales Slump

Day One: Acknowledge Your Slump and Take a Break

Take the day off. Go to the zoo and laugh at the monkeys. Go to a ball game. The mall and a movie. A relaxing drive in the country. Sit under a shade tree and enjoy a good book. Whatever may help you relax and cleanse your thoughts of frustration and tension. At the end of the day, get a good night's sleep.

Day Two: Begin Using a Complete Psycho-Cybernetics Mental Conditioning Regimen

Beginning today, and everyday, put together and use a *Psycho-Cybernetics regimen*. Visit the Theater of Your Mind and rerun mental movies of your past successes and reinvigorate your Success Mechanism. Reaffirm a set of exciting goals. Select or create several new, strong affirmations you can use to reprogram the self-image.

Day Three: Put Together Your New Battle Plan

Marshall your very best resources. Who are your best, most loyal, profitable clients you can call on first each day, count on for a positive experience, and confidently ask for referrals? Who are the prospects you've been cultivating, who are most likely to be ready to buy? Assemble a strong assault plan for the next two days. Plan intense, high-energy activity. Allocate every minute productively. Take a "blitz" approach to making things happen. Get into action, too. Get on the phone and set up those appointments. Focus entirely on what you *can* do; do not waste any mental energy on things you cannot control.

Day Four: Massive Action!

One of America's finest lecturers on personal development and success, Jim Rohn talks about the principle of *massive* action. Jim says that if you go and spend a week with a top performer in just about any field, you will walk away saying "No wonder he's so successful. Look at *everything* he does!" So that is the kind of day you want to have today and tomorrow. If an observer was watching your every movement, with you every minute, at the end of the day he or she would say about you: "It's no wonder she's so successful. Look at everything she does!"

Day Five: Harvest!

This is the first day of your new "boom period" in selling. You can start reaping the best harvest ever from all your efforts. You have every reason and right to anticipate successful results today. Follow-up confidently on past meetings, leads and contacts.

High Performers' Secret of Resiliency

When pro football coaches and key players, like quarterbacks or defensive corners are asked what quality is most important to success in the game, many say "very short memories." When a quarterback throws an interception or a corner gets badly beat by a pass receiver, he has to forget it, and gear up to perform on the very next play. Actually, I would say he has to instantly forgive and forget. This is resiliency.

Ego can drive you to win; desire for achievement can drive you to win; occasionally even desperation can drive you to win. But resiliency is necessary to *keep winning*. Ironically, ego can also prevent you from winning. Desire for achievement can even create frustration and stress that interferes with success. But resiliency always contributes to winning.

"It's no wonder he's so successful.

Look at everything he does!"

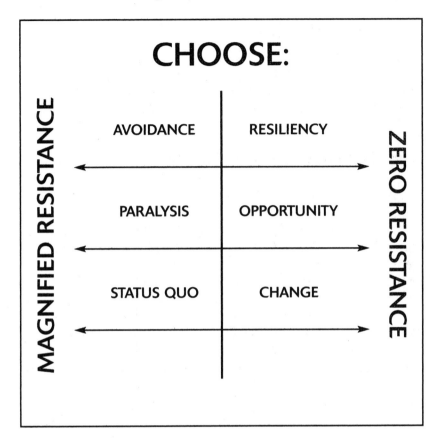

In many instances, a sales slump represents the decline of resiliency. When a salesperson gets into a slump, he/she can often be observed avoiding confrontation, procrastinating, reducing the quantity of activity. Finds it more difficult to bounce back from refusal and frustration, and avoids it. Of course, logic says it'd be better to turn up the activity a notch or two, redouble efforts, and play through the slump faster. But that requires great resiliency.

Resiliency can be programmed into the self-image. You need to create an image of yourself as the kind of person who is immune to temporary disappointments or setbacks, who can withstand occasional tough times with dignity and calm confidence, and bounce back quickly from adversity. Think about some of the noticeably resilient people you know, or know of from the news.

Donald Trump and Merv Griffin, business adversaries, have both exhibited great resiliency in their careers. Before them, Conrad Hilton, incredibly resilient, and his autobiography, *Be My Guest*, is a study in resiliency. Kathie Lee Gifford, who in 1996 came under enormous criticism and media attacks for having her line of women's clothing made by child laborers, quickly bounced back as a respected crusader for assertive enforcement of child labor laws and changes in U.S. import policies, featuring her testimony before the U.S. Congress. The actor Christopher Reeve suffered a terrible accident, spinal cord injury, and is fighting back from near total paralysis from the neck down. He admits to having contemplated suicide. But he has since proved remarkably resilient. He is earning excellent fees as a professional speaker, working to raise funds and facilitate research for spinal cord injuries, and in 1996 was a featured speaker at the Democratic National Convention.

Everybody has an experience of resiliency. There *are* times in your past when you have been resilient. As a child, when you fell over trying to ride your bicycle, did you get right back on? In Little League, did you miss an easy fly ball, but play again the next day and stop a difficult line drive to win a game? Were you ever told you lacked talent in a particular area, then proved your critic wrong? In your selling career, did you rebound from a very disappointing experience, beat out of an account by a competitor, and secure an even bigger account? Recall every example of resiliency from your past and present them all to your self-image at once, and tell yourself: "Look, I've been pretty resilient throughout my life. I clearly have the ability to bounce back quickly. Now I'm going to strengthen and emphasize this characteristic. I'm the kind of person who takes a hit and bounces right back up, stronger than ever." You can be like that Eveready bunny; you just keep going and going and going. Or the old Timex watch slogan; it takes a licking and keeps on ticking. Plug all *those* pictures into your self-image.

Chapter 6

How to Be a Master Closer

I get the appointment with the right decision maker, I deliver a killer presentation, I get favorable response, but when it comes to outright asking for the order, putting the contract on the table, I turn to mush. Why?

Closing a sale is what ultimately separates professional salespeople from professional conversationalists. Many otherwise effective sales professionals "wimp out" when it comes to closing the sale. It is obviously easier and less confrontive to let the presentation peter out, and to leave with a pleasant "maybe" than to confront rejection and the finality of a "no." Salespeople with weak self-images choose that easier option more often than not.

One of the top experts in teaching dentists how to sell, Greg Stanley of Whitehall Management, says that the biggest single difference between the dentist who sells two million dollars a year of full treatments, cosmetic dentistry, and other services and the many dentists who struggle to do a tenth of that is "confrontational tolerance." Greg says the high-income dentist has, for dentists, an uncharacteristically high tolerance for direct, straightforward confrontation. All Master Closers share this high level of confrontational tolerance. In fact, many thrive on the confrontation.

Where does such a high level of confrontational tolerance come from? I'm here to tell you it is a representation of the strongest, healthiest self-image you can build.

111

In the famous play *Death of a Salesman*, playwright Arthur Miller described the salesman, Willy Loman, this way:

> Willy was a salesman. And for a salesman there is no rock bottom to the life. He don't put a bolt to a nut, he don't tell you the law or give you medicine. He's a man way out there in the blue, riding on a smile and a shoeshine. And when they start not smiling back—that's an earthquake. And then you get yourself a couple of spots on your hat, and you're finished.

What a depressing, frightening, limiting view of the salesperson! This view says that, as a salesperson, you are getting by with smoke and mirrors, completely vulnerable to fickle clientele, easily destroyed, with no control over your destiny. Arthur Miller's character was desperate to be liked, at any price, out of pure, unadulterated fear. If we were to perform a detailed autopsy on Willy Loman's self-image, we would uncover nothing but scar tissue. Willy could not have been a Master Closer.

Well, the days of "smile and shoeshine selling" are long gone. Today's customers are smarter, more demanding of value, and the process of selling is more scientific and professional than ever before. Today's sales professionals are rarely "lone rangers" either. Most are supported by sophisticated technology, well-managed organizations, advertising, direct marketing programs and other assets. But the most important thing for today's sales pro seeking Master Closer status is the same as it was twenty, thirty or forty years ago; the opposite of the Willy Loman attitude; a strong self-image.

Ten Characteristics of Master Closers

Over the years, I've had many opportunities to visit at length with Master Closers in many different selling fields and organizations, and I've taken careful note of how their strong self-images manifest themselves in actual behavior. Here are the 10 behavioral characteristics I've found in common, in all Master Closers:

1. The Master Closer shows no fear. The Master Closer is never pushy and does not resort to obvious "hard sell" tactics. These are the signs of weakness, desperation and fear exhibited by a salesperson who is so vulnerable to rejection and feelings of inadequacy that he or she feels compelled to make a sale at any cost. The Master Closer is confident and relaxed, and lets the conversation take its own course and move at its own pace. The Master Closer wants the prospect to buy, not to be rushed or pushed. He or she welcomes questions and objections, confident that airing them and answering them will advance, not derail the sale.

2. The Master Closer is not selling just for the commission. Salespeople who are "in it only for the money" may be able to close like the dickens for short spurts, but they cannot sustain it, because their activity is not reinforcing a positive self-image. The Master Closer has profound, genuine belief in the value of what he or she is selling to the prospect. High commissions and high closing percentages generally reflect the sales professional's sincere commitment to his/her product or service and sincere concern for the customer. The Master Closer thrives on the entire process of matching the right people with the right product.

3. The Master Closer never gets down on him- or herself. The Critic Within is very well controlled. The Master Closer never beats him- or herself about the shoulders with "If only I'd said this". . . "How could I not have noticed that?". . .and all the other after-the-fact "if's" one can dwell on after missing a sale. The Master Closer may take mental note of an error or two, but never fashions them into a club to pound him- or herself into the dirt with.

4. The Master Closer is very organized and straightforward in asking for action. You'll never hear a Master Closer use a weak, timid question like "Well, what do you think?" Most Master Closers boil down their propositions to two or three choices, and directly ask the prospect to pick one. They use power phrases like: "Here's how we will get started."

Here's one example. Former Secretary of State Henry Kissinger once told of a reaction he received from the late Chairman Mao Tse-tung of China.

"What do you want from us?' Chairman Mao asked bluntly.

"We seek nothing but your friendship," Kissinger replied diplomatically.

The shrewd Chinese leader stuck with bluntness and said, "If you want nothing, you shouldn't be here. If I sought nothing from you, I would not have invited you to come here."

A prospective customer or client with half a brain knows you are in his or her presence to make a sale. Not directly asking for what you want accomplishes nothing. It may cause the prospect to lose respect for you. After all, if you aren't confident enough to tell him/her to buy, why should the prospect be confident enough to buy?

Master Closers exhibit no hesitancy or reluctance about asking for the order.

5. The Master Closer understands the prospect has doubts, fears, the temptation to avoid confrontation and decision, too. Just as sales professionals must overcome these demons, everybody has them— the corporate CEO or the small shopkeeper or the consumer.

I once counseled a salesman who was seeing plenty of good prospects but rarely made a sale. After some conversation, he confessed, "I don't want to be perceived as some pushy salesman. I respect my customers' intelligence. They can make and should make their own choices and decisions. If they are ready to buy, they should say so." This deluded fellow was lugging around a Willy Loman complex the size of an elephant. He wanted to be liked more than anything else, including closing sales. Master Closers want to close sales more than anything else in the world, even being liked. He believed his job was to present information. Master Closers know that their job is to close sales. He had no faith in himself and his ability to control the outcomes of his meetings, and believed it was up to the prospect to determine the outcome. The Master Closer has total confidence in his ability to control the outcomes, and believes it is up to him to do so, so he acts accordingly.

The Master Closer knows that the prospect wants him/her to be firm, convinced, and reassuring, to help the prospect act rather than avoid or postpone a decision.

6. The Master Closer is immune to rejection. In other words, he/she never takes prospects' questions, objections or even ultimate refusal to act personally. These events do not penetrate the self-image.

I happened to be on the set where a television program was being filmed once, thanks to a friend who was a producer. I watched as a stunt man making a leap from one building's rooftop to another misjudged the jump, hesitated, stumbled, and sloppily fell into the airbag in the street below. I knew that the entire stunt would have to be filmed again. And I suspected that the stunt man was pretty embarrassed by his mistake. While the crew set up to do it all over again, the producer and the stunt man came over to the table where the coffee pot sat, and where I was standing. The producer introduced the stunt man to me and I to him. I asked him how he felt about the faux pas he had just made.

"Oh, that's nothing," he said. "To a young guy just starting out, a rookie, it might mean something. But I'm one of the three best stunt men working in television today. A screw-up like that is just business as usual to me, like a really good secretary hitting the wrong key on the typewriter and having to go and get an eraser. No big deal."

Master Closers react the same way to missed sales.

7. Master Closers are unaffected by resistance. They do not fear prospects' questions or objections, in fact, they welcome them as "helpers" in making the sale. This is a point I've made elsewhere in this book, but it is a behavioral trait exhibited by all Master Closers, so I'd be remiss to omit it here. Some salespeople are like dumb, stubborn sailors who, when the wind turns against them, buck up against it and stall or even capsize their boats. The Master Closer is quick to adapt, to turn and capture the changing wind as an ally.

8. Master Closers avoid all negative influences and distractions. The Master Closer is totally focused on closing sales. You rarely catch a Master Closer hanging around the water cooler or coffee pot, joining in the day's gripe session about the weather or the city's inept team or whatever else is complaint du jour.

9. Master Closers are competitive yet remarkably stress free. How can this be? Because the Master Closer enjoys competing with him- or herself, to better his/her best, to best his/her own records, but is largely unconcerned with competing with or comparing him- or herself to others.

I once had a salesperson come to see me, and tell me that he was making a good living but absolutely miserable where he was working. Here's a short portion of our conversation:

> MM: Why are you so miserable?
>
> BILL: The competition is driving me crazy. We have twenty salespeople at the dealership. There's a big board in the coffee break room, and each salesperson's statistics are up there for everybody to see.
>
> They track sales, dollars of each sale, profit margins of each sale, totals, and the manager updates them just about every time somebody makes a sale, sometimes ten times a day.
>
> MM: And why does that bother you so much?
>
> BILL: Dr. Maltz, the pressure is intolerable. I'm always worried about who's getting ahead of me. Who's doing better than I am. I check that darned board four or five times a day. I even dream about that board at night.
>
> MM: Let's forget the scoreboard for a second. Where do you usually end up at the end of the month?
>
> BILL: Well, I'm one of the top salespeople there. In the last six months, I was number one overall twice, number two three times, and number three once.
>
> MM: What about for the year?
>
> BILL: Last year, I was number one in quantity of sales, number two in gross dollars, number two in profit margin . . . and, by the way, number one in customer satisfaction ratings.

MM: With that track record, how difficult would it be for you to get a position at another dealership?

BILL: Easy. Some try to recruit me now. I could go to any city in America and have a great job in thirty minutes.

MM: So, let me see: you are a top performer. You are obviously respected by your current employer and peers. You are liked by your customers. And you have tremendous security, because you would be eagerly welcomed by just about any company in your industry. Yet you are feeling miserable every day because of an inanimate object, a chalkboard on a wall, which you must go out of your way to look at, like a hiker deliberately climbing over a high fence to get into poison ivy. What do you make of all that?

BILL: Well, when you put it that way, it sounds a little silly.

MM: Let me ask you another question: In the last six months, have there been any days where you've been beaten badly on the board? Been number 5 or 6 or worse?

BILL: Sure. Everybody has off days. I'm no exception.

MM: Yet at the end of the month, when all the days are combined, you're a consistent winner.

BILL: Yes.

MM: Let's try an experiment. I want you to do two things for the coming month. First, I want you to set goals of your own, for your own sales, margins, and so on, and break them down into daily goals—where you need to be at the end of each day. And I want you to make up your own chalkboard as a chart on paper, to measure yourself against those daily goals. Second, I want you to completely ignore the chalkboard in the break room. Don't look at it. Don't peek. Don't even go in there. I know the suspense will be intense, but you must try to resist the temptation. Put a little coffee pot in your own office so you have no reason to go into that break room. Will you try this experiment?

BILL: It's going to be tough. But I'll do my best.

MM: Good. And when the urge to go look occurs, I want you, instead, to lean back in your chair, close your eyes, go into the Theater of Your Mind and run little minimovies of your happiest customers getting their new cars, of you getting awards at last year's banquet, and other things like that. Finish a movie. Applaud. Then go back to work.

About two months later, Bill dropped by my office, a big smile on his face. "I didn't make it all the way through the month," he confessed. "I peeked a few times. But I did get the message. By focusing on my goals instead of what everybody else was doing, I felt a lot less stress and I was more productive. I did more telephone prospecting than I've probably done in any month before. And at the end of the month, I hit or did better than every goal I'd set. Now I've compiled stats on my best months and I compete against those and measure my daily progress toward my goals."

Bill is stepping up to Master-Closer status.

10. Master Closers celebrate success. Without letting ego become obnoxious, Master Closers reward themselves and celebrate their successes without apology or guilt. I am always surprised to see people who are doing well but are dour. Your self-image is strengthened by victory. The *feeling* of victory is important.

The Ten Characteristics of Master Closers

1. The Master Closer shows no fear.

2. The Master Closer is not selling just for the commission.

3. The Master Closer never gets down on him- or herself.

4. The Master Closer is very organized and straightforward in asking for action.

5. The Master Closer understands the prospect has doubts, fears, the temptation to avoid confrontation and decision, too.

6. The Master Closer is immune to rejection.

7. Master Closers are unaffected by resistance.

8. Master Closers avoid all negative influences and distractions.

9. Master Closers are competitive yet remarkably stress free.

10. Master Closers celebrate success.

Chapter 7

How to Enjoy Happiness and Peace of Mind as a Professional Salesperson

You are a good sales professional. You are knowledgeable, skilled, talented, ambitious, persistent. You are successful. But there is a dark cloud looming overhead. For some reason, even as you are earning more, you seem to be enjoying it less. While success is obtainable, joy is elusive. The surge of enthusiasm, pride and satisfaction you used to feel when you closed a big sale or secured an important new account doesn't happen anymore. You find it harder to shake off a stressful day. There are days when you even wonder if you should be in sales at all.

A woman, Barbara, came in to my office to see me. She explained that she was trying to develop a career selling real estate, but was meeting with a lot of resistance at home, from her husband and family, and felt it was wearing her down.

MM: Why is your family so resistant to your career?

BARBARA: Well, they don't come out and say it exactly like that, but I get the hints. They're not very subtle.

MM: All right, tell me about the hints.

BARBARA: Every once in a while, I'll have a late appointment to show a house or make a listing presentation and I won't be able to get home to make dinner. My husband usually calls for pizza delivery or brings home a bucket of chicken, and when I get home he jokes about being Mr. Mom and having to slave away in the kitchen after a hard day's work.

MM: What else?

BARBARA: Both my husband and my oldest son, he's 17, have asked me a number of times why I want to put myself through all this. After all, my husband makes very good money and we have no need of my earning an income. Lately my husband has been bringing up things like how much a neighbor enjoys her volunteer work at the hospital. Or maybe my redecorating our house; would I like to handle that? That sort of thing. I also notice that arguments over little, really inconsequential things are occurring with greater frequency, especially in weeks when I am especially busy with real estate.

MM: Well, how are things going for you in real estate?

BARBARA: It's quite difficult in the beginning. I haven't built up a client base, so there are no referrals. I have to solicit strangers. It's very slow-going and frustrating. Also, I'm not a young woman anymore—I've been at home raising kids for almost ten years—so a long Saturday at an Open House leaves me bushed.

MM: So why *do* you want to put yourself through this?

BARBARA: I always thought I'd be good at selling. I wanted to try and do something all my own, on my own. The kids will soon be grown and I don't want to just putter around the house by myself. Even when Harry retires soon, he'll go play golf, which I don't like, work in his wood shop in the garage, and so forth, so I'll want something to do. I thought I could work hard for a few years, learn the ropes, get good, build up a clientele, then cut back, do it in my spare time, just ten or twenty hours a week. Right now, I've put several listings on the books and I'm proud of that. I enjoy the give-and-take of selling. It makes me feel happy to accomplish something like listing a home. So even though it is difficult going right now, I also like the sense of accomplishment, I like the people I work with and I feel like I'm on the right track for my future.

MM:　When you come home after a day of this, what do you do? What do you say? Think about this. Tell me in detail.

BARBARA:　Hmm. Well, yesterday, it was very hot. I was in and out of the car a lot, going to appointments. I had a 6:00 listing appointment that didn't work out very well. When I came home, I was tired, a bit frustrated. I was preoccupied with thinking about how I could have done that presentation differently. I think I was short, kind of barked at Johnny for making too much noise in the living room. I spoke with my husband briefly, then went upstairs, took a shower, a couple aspirin, and dozed off in a chair in the bedroom.

MM:　Would that be unusual?

BARBARA:　Well, I'm not like that everyday. But I guess it's not unusual either.

MM:　You just gave me a message about your selling career that was positive, optimistic and upbeat. You told me about a feeling of pride and fulfillment from your accomplishments. But what was the message you gave your husband and family when you came home last night, grumpy and fatigued?

BARBARA:　I never thought about it like that.

MM:　Is it possible that their resistance to what you are doing is really concern for you? Based on what they see about your activity? They don't see your happiness after making a good presentation. They only see your fatigue and frustration. The messages you are giving them are very different from the message you gave me. Maybe you are creating the resistance.

BARBARA: Maybe you are on to something.

MM: Let me try something else out on you. Is it possible that one of the reasons you decided to start your sales career was to get attention, to be noticed and to be important? After many years of marriage, spouses tend to stop giving attention to each other. Your husband might bury his nose in the newspaper rather than talk to you at breakfast. And kids take everything mother does for granted. So a sales career offers a chance to be important, to get recognition. But if you are looking for attention at home—well, a lot of people find that the best way to get that is by complaining rather than being cheerful. By being stressed out or exhausted or ill. By behaving like a martyr.

BARBARA: I don't like hearing that. I don't think I'm like that at all.

MM: Maybe not. Let me ask you another question: Have you ever sat down with your family and told them the things you told me, about why you want to carve out a career for yourself selling real estate?

BARBARA: Not exactly.

MM: Here's what I think. I think the resistance to your career that you are feeling hanging heavy in your home like thick smog hanging over the city is quite real, but that you are the one cranking up the smog machine. I'll bet you are manufacturing the resistance. I hope you'll think about that. And I'm going to write out a little note, a prescription on this prescription pad. I want you to somehow fasten it to the visor, mirror, or dashboard of your car and read it every time you get out of your car, but especially when you get home at the end of the day, before going into your home.

On the prescription slip, I wrote: *Rx: Think! What message am I going to communicate now about my selling career?*

And that was that. A few months went by before I accidentally bumped into this woman again; she was in the audience at a
sales conference of real estate agents, where I was a guest speaker
on the subject of Psycho-Cybernetics. On the break, she took me
aside and told me how well things were going.

> "I made a point of shaking off my fatigue before going home
> each night, even if that meant stopping at a coffee shop for an
> iced tea or just sitting in my parked car for a few minutes to try
> and relax. Then when I went into my house, I took time to visit
> with my kids, talked with my husband and talked about the
> positive things that had gone on that day and, although it was
> difficult to do, how I felt about accomplishing something.
> Gradually, everybody stopped complaining or hinting that I
> ought to quit. For my birthday, the kids chipped in and got me
> my ticket to this seminar!"

Selling *is* hard work. Often there are long hours, calls and
paperwork brought home. You may be fatigued, frustrated, worried—
or, I hope thanks to the ideas in this book—creatively preoccupied
during an evening, mentally preparing for an important presentation
the next day. All of this can be misconstrued by your family, even by
your own Servo-Mechanism. If you are grumbling and complaining,
irritable and apparently unhappy a lot of the time, your family will
resent your career for making you so; your Servo-Mechanism may
try to get you out of the unpleasant situation by destroying your sales
career! You must ask yourself: What message am I giving to my family, and to my self-image, about my selling career?

Here are two simple ideas: If you are happy in your selling
career, show it. That's one. Two, if you are *not* happy, do something
about it.

Why You Might *Not* Enjoy Selling

If you are not thoroughly enjoying selling—not just the desirable
outcome of the high income, but the actual process, the day-to-day
activity of selling—then you will gradually take power away from
your Success Mechanism, empower your Failure Mechanism, and

find it increasingly difficult to force yourself to do what is necessary to be successful. Before you know it, you'll be stuck in a slump. Here are the chief reasons why you may not enjoy selling:

1. Skill deficiencies. It's difficult to enjoy doing something you don't do well! Maybe you haven't had sufficient training in one or more of the skills of selling, such as prospecting or presenting or closing. Learn the skills! Master the skills!

It is interesting to me that most salespeople want and expect to harvest a "professional" income from their career but rarely think about investing the kind of time, earnest study and money in their professional education as most other professionals must. Also, when I ask salespeople if they have rehearsed their presentations as great actors, comedians, entertainers, and speakers do, or role-played their presentations in order to smooth out the imperfections, I usually get "no, not really" as an answer. "Mastery" and "winging it" do not go together.

2. Esteem deficiencies. Maybe you simply have a negative feeling about selling. Did you once want to be something else but you feel you've "settled for" a career in selling? Does your father, mother, or brother look down on salespeople? Are you fixated on the media stereotypes of the lying, cheating, scheming, disreputable salesperson? You must alter your basic perception of what a sales professional is. Here are some affirmations that may help you:

- Selling is an honorable profession worthy of my best efforts
- To sell is to serve
- I enable my clients to solve their problems, achieve their goals and add value to their lives
- Sales professionals are the driving force of the American economy. Nothing happens until somebody sells something!

3. Burn-out and boredom. Maybe you're an "old pro," and you've been doing the same things the same way over and over and over again, so you are bored with the routine, maybe even cynical about your clientele or business. You'll have to shake things up. Seek out and experiment with new ideas and new methods. Take on a novice and be his or her mentor and role model. Set new goals that excite your Success Mechanism. Reinvigorate yourself by turning work into a game. Set daily or weekly benchmarks and tie little rewards to each one.

4. Integrity conflict. This may be the biggest single cause of unhappiness and frustration in selling that there is. If you are being asked to do things or have to do things to make sales that are in conflict with your personal integrity, it'll be impossible to be happy over the long haul. You must find a way to sell and an environment to sell in that you can feel good about. You should not only feel good about the commission check you get but about what you did to get it.

One time while speaking for a large group of Met Life agents, I was having lunch in the coffee shop and a young man asked if he could join me. "I'm looking forward to hearing your speech," he said, "because, to tell you the truth, I'm not sure of my future selling insurance. And I'm embarrassed when people ask what I do for a living."

Despite that statement, this young man, Tony, epitomized success and professionalism. He was very well-dressed. Articulate. As I queried him about his career, I found he was earning over $150,000 annually. Yet he had lost his enthusiasm for his career, his company and his industry.

That day I gave my speech under the title "My Momma Wanted Me to Be a Doctor, But Here I am, Selling Insurance." I talked about "career esteem" and how it affected the self-image. Without naming him, I made Tony my poster boy for unhappiness in selling. I challenged the agents to recruit themselves into their business, to write down at least 50 good reasons to choose a career in life insurance sales versus any other possible career and to write down 50 fresh or restated short, medium and long-term career goals. (You need to "re-recruit yourself" into your business everyday!)

Tony is not alone. The sales world is full of salespeople walking around "shut down," fatigued, bored, burnt-out, without genuine enthusiasm. In social situations, they feel embarrassed or hesitant to tell others what they do for a living. They are forever questioning their career choice. If you are in this group, let this chapter be a giant alarm bell and wake-up call for you. You cannot just "go through the motions" in selling like you may be able to do in less demanding and accountable jobs.

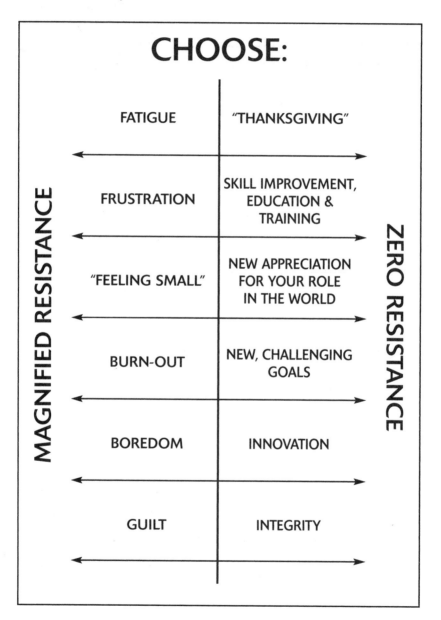

Frank Bettger wrote a book called *How I Raised Myself From Failure to Success in Selling* that demonstrates the enormous importance of sincere enthusiasm to the sales professional. If you don't have it, you've got to get it! It's natural to daydream every once in a while about doing other things, or think how your life might be different if, at some past fork in the road, you had taken another turn. But, on par, if you had the opportunity to do it all over again, and you wouldn't choose the selling career you now find yourself in, then maybe you should make a change now. But first step back and carefully examine what it is that you do, the quality you represent, the clients who appreciate you and depend on you, the opportunities in your hands. Decide: Is this something I can get excited about and energized over? If so, dig in, and excel. If not, change.

How Underselling Robs Some Salespeople of Maximum Earnings

A sales manager with a large company told me that he was absolutely perplexed by the poor performance of one of his representatives. He told me that analysis of the accounts Al had and regularly sold to clearly indicated their usage volume of the products should be two to three times higher, so these accounts had to be splitting their business between two or three vendors. I met with Al. Here's part of our conversation:

MM: Management showed me records that show your income's about average, right in the middle, yet I'm told you have a very valuable and productive territory. Are you interested in increasing your sales?

AL: Of course. Who wouldn't be? But really, I do everything there is to do in selling and servicing these accounts. You can ask any of these purchasing guys—they all like me. I get along well with all of them.

MM: Do you think that's important?

AL: What?

MM: These relationships. Being liked by the purchasing people.

AL: Well, sure. People buy people, not products; that's my motto.

MM: What if I told you that some pretty good analysis of your key accounts says they're splitting up their purchases between you and other competitors? Why do you think you don't get all their business? Or more of it?

AL: I'd like to punch whoever said that in the nose!

MM: Really? Why?

AL: Hey nobody knows what it's like out there in the field unless they're there. No analyst or consultant. Or you either. It's tough. Competition's tough. I've got to walk a tightrope between selling and pushing too hard.

MM: I want you to go home and think about something, okay?

AL: Okay.

MM: First, a picture: you are on the beach, at the edge of the ocean. The ocean extends for as far as you can see. And it is deeper than you can see, if you wade out just a few yards from shore. Above the ocean, in the sky, the fluffy white clouds have spelled out the words *unlimited abundance*. Next to you on the sand there is a teaspoon, a tablespoon, a cup, and a bucket. Second, I want you to seriously think about each of your accounts and how much you sell to them. I want you to entertain the possibility that you are underselling these accounts, and ask yourself why. Call me in a week or so.

About a week later, Al called me on the phone and said, "I got it. I think I've been underselling these accounts for years and I've figured out why. I don't like pushy, high-pressure salespeople, so

I've bent over backwards *not* to be seen that way by others. I want them to like me, not see me as just another pushy salesman. I've turned myself into a timid mouse. Since I'm not asking for the business and not making a case for it, I'm not getting it."

"Al," I said, "the ocean doesn't care if you use a teaspoon or a bucket."

A few months later, I heard from Al and from his sales manager. Al had increased volume in his territory by nearly 40%.

Are you underselling? There are many ways to do it. Small business owners, service providers and professionals will undercharge and underprescribe in fear of being perceived as too pushy, too sales-y, too greedy, too this or too that. Salespeople undersell and hold back from asking for more business, like Al did. Or they get weak-kneed when it comes time to ask for the order for fear of being seen as too pushy.

In almost every instance, you will judge yourself more harshly on these counts than will clients, customers, patients or prospects. Consider silencing your Critic Within for a while and testing these limits, of pushing a bit harder, speaking a bit more forcefully, reaching for slightly more ambitious-sized orders and see what happens. Give your market a chance to tell you whether or not you are stuck using a teaspoon or might be able to use a bucket.

How Your Self-Image Defines Just How Much You Can Earn

Simply put, your self-image defines the "Realm of the Possible." You cannot outperform your own self-image, no matter how hard you try, no matter how much willpower, grit, determination or motivation you have. The self-image says "Stop!" and you stop. The self-image defines how easy or difficult it is for you to meet people, secure appointments, build rapport, present, convince, and close sales; whether or not you'll be on time or tardy; how much money you can make; and whether or not you'll be happy making it.

Some years ago, I encountered a salesman who had skyrocketed to the top earnings level in a particular company. Only months after joining this sales organization, he was earning a remarkable income, many weeks over $10,000. Then it seemed like he ran into a brick wall and crashed to the ground. His earnings dropped below a $1,000 a week and stayed there no matter what he did. It turns out that his father, also a salesman his entire life, had never earned more than $100,000 in a year—roughly $10,000 a month. When this young "pup" started making that much in a *week*, he started questioning himself: "Wait a minute," his self-image said, "what's this $10,000 a week stuff? Pop never made that much in a whole *month*! Do you really think you're that much better than he is? This can't last." To make matters worse, his fiancee actually became alarmed at how well he was doing. She kept warning him that it couldn't continue as it was, so they'd better save all the money they could for that inevitable "rainy day." She even expressed the idea that it was impossible to make that kind of money honestly. Was he sure what he was doing was on the up-and-up? His own ingrained, past programming of what a top salesman was supposed to earn, his fiancee's fears, and his own uncertainty ganged up on his self-image and beat it back down to the size of a small potato. His income quickly followed.

The amount on your commission check is conceived in your self-image and written in pencil by your Servo-Mechanism before it is inked in by your sales manager.

How Your Self-Image Regulates Peace of Mind Like a Thermostat Regulates Room Temperature

Another man I know was consistently earning over a quarter-of-a-million dollars a year, but was clearly miserable. He drank too often and too much. Smoked like a fiend. Ate poorly. It always looked like his stomach was attacking him, even though he ate antacid tablets like candy. He was committing suicide on the installment plan. He initially came to see me, to have the bags and creases under his eyes surgically removed, so he could look younger. I told him they'd be back there again in just a few years if he kept torturing himself everyday. As I got to know him better, I discovered he was committed to earning a top income but that it required long hours and involved so much pressure, he was always exhausted when he arrived home, and was building up a large amount of guilt over never spending time with his young son. He couldn't have made it more difficult: they lived in a ritzy suburb a good hour's commute from his city office, so he spent two hours everyday in his car, and was just about guaranteed to arrive home at his son's bedtime every night. He often had to attend first-thing-in-the-morning meetings, so he was out of the house by 7:00 A.M., barely gulping a cup of coffee and saying "good morning" to his wife and son.

His self-image featured "poor father" and "poor husband" right up there with "top salesman." His self-image induced self-punishment refused to let him enjoy his success.

Instead of surgically removing the bags under his eyes, I talked with him about the baggage he was asking his self-image to lug around, and how it was getting heavier by the minute. I suggested he invest the day of recuperation that would follow his surgery in checking into a hotel room, unplugging the phone and the TV, and just thinking about how he might reorganize his life for the better, to liberate his self-image from the piling on of guilt, and to derive some joy and fulfillment from his accomplishments.

Do these two people seem extreme to you? Maybe they are. But you will be well served by taking a few moments to seriously question yourself, about what may be going on in your self-image, sabotaging your peace of mind.

Fortunately, the second fellow found himself and his self-respect during a day alone, in the solitude of a hotel room. He sat down with his wife and son, had a serious talk, and, together they came up with a "battle plan" to attack the thieves of their quality of life and peace of mind. Over the next year, they found and purchased a new home in a suburb thirty minutes closer to the city, slashing his commute time by half. (In a year, that's 365 hours—the equivalent of 9 work weeks!) He set aside Wednesday as a "work from home day," and used the time from 8:00 to 4:00 to be available for phone calls, do the entire week's correspondence and paperwork, and make telephone prospecting calls. At noon, he took a break and had a pleasant lunch with his wife. At 4:00, he spent the rest of the afternoon with his son, and was able to get to some of his ball games for the first time. Wednesday evening, he was relaxed and could enjoy the evening with his family. Once a month, he took Fridays off and planned three-day family weekends.

After a year or so, he visited with me, and told me his income had been reduced by about $50,000 a year as a result of these changes, but that he considered it a very small price to pay for his peace of mind.

There's an excellent book I recommend, *Grow Rich With Peace of Mind*, in which Napoleon Hill describes a similar journey to peace of mind.

Many people say that they want "peace of mind." If that is something you desire, you have to *be* the kind of person who has peace of mind, first in your self-image. This is not a difficult process to understand. Here are the steps:

1. Define the kind of person who has peace of mind. What are his/her characteristics? Beliefs? Behaviors? Does this person have a good sense of humor? Compete but never compare him- or herself to others? Deal with others honestly? Respond to adversity calmly? Refuse to let others' pettiness anger him/her? Get in your mind, or preferably on paper, a very good, detailed description and vivid picture of this person. A list of the "factors" that make him/her the kind of person who has peace of mind.

2. Use those "factors" to set new "thought goals," "emotion goals" and "behavior goals" for yourself. Pick the three, four or five you feel are most important.

3. Turn these goals into affirmations, such as: "I am the kind of person who stays cool and calm and thoughtful and creative in times of adversity or crisis, even when all around me, others succumb to tension, pressure, worry or anxiety. I'm a cool cat." Create a little mental picture you can "pop up" instantly to remind yourself of your affirmation. In this case, it might be a cat wearing a beret-style hat and sunglasses, peacefully dozing in a recliner chair, with jazz music playing on the stereo, an iced beverage in a glass by his or her side—if you will, a "cool cat." The affirmation and the picture are the tools you'll use to practice the desired behavior.

4. Go into the Theater of Your Mind at least once a day, to run mental movies of times in the past when you've exhibited and benefited from the desired behavior, as well as of times to come when you use the desired behavior successfully, with them all seen as present tense. Create vivid detail.

5. Find a good relaxation exercise you like and are comfortable with and use it for a mini-mental vacation once or twice a day, to defuse whatever tension builds up. There are several in the book *Psycho-Cybernetics*. Some people report excellent results from the use of self-hypnosis or subliminal programming cassettes for daily relaxation.* Also, most people find that some form of daily physical exercise is valuable not only for its own merits, but as a means of releasing stress. A good, brisk walk can do wonders!

Be Proud to Be a Sales Professional

Many people say that they "just want to be happy." The process for creating happiness is much the same as the one I've just outlined for creating peace of mind. However, especially for the sales professional, I believe that pride and happiness are closely linked. How can you be happy in a career you aren't proud of?

Pride is important. I once found myself sitting at a lunch counter next to a New York police officer. He was joking with the waitress, sharing a cartoon in the newspaper with the fellow seated on his other side, and generally having a good time. I had read the newspaper front page that morning and found it full of crime, political chaos, and economic bad news. I said to the policeman:" If you don't mind my asking about it, I'm fascinated with your happy attitude. As a police officer, you must deal with negativity all day long. Criminals, people who are impoverished, spouses fighting with one another. If you go by this newspaper, the city is crashing down around our ears and you are wading through that rubble. Certainly the streets are dirty and dangerous. The traffic jams are unbearable. So how is it that you are so cheerful?"

---

*Special creative Psycho-Cybernetics subliminal cassettes are available from The Psycho-Cybernetics Foundation: Phone (602) 265-1922.

He thought for a second, then said, "You know, you're right about everything you said. A lot of what I deal with every day is very ugly and frustrating. But when I put on this uniform and badge every morning and check myself in the mirror, I'm proud to be on the job. I know the department's had its scandals, but it also has a long, proud tradition. Last year, I saved the life of a guy being assaulted in an alley, helped a frightened woman give birth to a baby, and stopped a robbery in progress at a very nice couple's little store. I'm proud of doing those things. So I guess I can be cheerful even in these uncheerful times because of that pride."

May I give you some raw material for *your* self-image? The average dentist, chiropractor, podiatrist, corporate executive, college dean or professor, or lawyer might be surprised to see the bankbooks of a great many sales professionals in insurance and securities, real estate, automobiles, industrial chemicals, even multilevel or network marketing as well as dozens of other fields. I personally know many people in every one of those industries earning over $250,000 a year. In sales fields like real estate, for example, a woman can come into the business after ten years as a stay-at-home-mom and, after only a couple years, be earning as much as her doctor is, after 10 years of college and 20 years of practice. In insurance, a retired military officer can create a career and an income in less than five years that rivals that of a lawyer's, requiring eight years of college and many more years of building up a practice. In short, nobody's got anything on you when it comes to financial opportunity or stature.

What about value to society? Well, certainly the talented surgeon who saves life in the operating room, the school teacher who molds young minds, the police officer who puts his/her life at risk for our safety, these people all deserve our respect. But let's recognize that our society is a very complex weave of interdependence and interests, with every person playing a role of importance, significance, and value.

The police officer who may save your life tomorrow is there to do it because his/her life was saved last week by a bulletproof vest that was sold to the department by a sales representative. The prominent surgeon would be helpless without the sophisticated technology that was sold to the hospital by knowledgeable sales professionals in the medical products field. No person, family, company, or institution can long survive without the influence of countless sales professionals.

The insurance salesperson may be the brunt of jokes, but every one of the jokesters' families will be grateful to an insurance agent at some difficult time in the future, when that jokester is hospitalized, requires long term care or passes away. They will be very glad that their family's insurance agent took care of things appropriately.

The automobile salesperson may be the brunt of jokes, but I have some appreciation for them; as a plastic surgeon, I often provided people with operations not required by their physical health but very beneficial to their self-images. I know that often the auto salesperson does the same. He/she helps an individual find the automobile that fits the family budget, provides safe transport for the family, creates pride of ownership, and rewards hard work and achievement.

When a young couple pulls into the parents' driveway in their first new car, imagine their feelings of excitement and pride. When a hard-working man is able to trade in an old "beater" of a car and provide his family with a safer, shiny new minivan, that automobile salesperson has played a part in our great interweave of interests, and done it well. That auto salesperson has not only served that family honorably, but also contributed to the paychecks of all the support staff in the dealership, all the factory workers in Detroit, contributed to the dividends paid to the company's stockholders, including retirement and pension funds.

Believe me, if every sales professional stayed home in bed for just one week, our entire economy would grind to a halt and society would be in chaos.

What about skill and expertise? The top salespeople need give ground to no one in this department either. The top salespeople are psychologists, confidants, consultants, product engineers, business advisors, family advisors, and creative forces. The top salespeople develop comprehensive product knowledge, not only know their business but also the business of their clients. They develop remarkable understanding of human nature and behavior. The best salespeople solve problems for their clients or customers.

You may tell your self-image that the career you have chosen in selling is just as important, challenging, prestigious, and valuable as any other career. And you will be telling it the truth!

What Discomfort Robs You of Happiness in Selling?

Different people are robbed of happiness in selling by different things. I will give you one great example, then you can diagnose your own particular discomfort and heal it.

I once coached a salesman, John, who had been very actively involved in his community for a dozen years. He served on the boards of several charitable organizations, coached a Pop Warner football team, and was a church leader. However, he would never contact people he knew as a result of those activities to offer them his products and services, for fear that he'd be seen as unfairly trading on his community activism, as a "parasite" taking advantage of those situations. When pressed on this point, he told me he believed people would think he joined the civic activities purely for personal gain. When he came to see me, a new sales manager had come into the company, realized John had never worked his "warm market" of personal contacts, and was putting a lot of pressure on him to do so.

John derived great pride from his contributions to the community. His fear of having that pride undermined by having his motives falsely perceived was a growing, nagging discomfort robbing him of happiness in his selling career. Of course, his fear was completely irrational. After not prospecting in these groups for twelve years, how could anybody suspect him of being involved only to prospect? But when you are "inside" an irrational fear, it seems real and sensible.

Logically, he understood that his fear was irrational. He even acknowledged the obvious truth that many of these people who knew, respected and liked him were buying the products and services he sold from others only because they had no idea he sold them. How many of these people would prefer doing business with him? How many might even be puzzled that he had never asked them to do so? He acknowledged all this, but was still paralyzed by his fear and suffered monstrously as a result.

I suggested this for his discomfort: "John, I'll tell you what you can try. Just test it out on one or two people, three at the very most, then stop and don't do it anymore for a month. That'll be long enough for you to determine if peoples' attitudes have changed toward you. I want you to simply speak about the discomfort you are experiencing. Approach someone in your groups and say something like this: Bill, you and I have known each other for almost a dozen years. I've never mentioned it, but I'm in a business where I've been able to help a lot of families just like yours save small fortunes on their taxes and home mortgages. I haven't talked to you about what I do because I was worried that you would think I was involved in this charity just to prospect for clients. But I've been thinking that over and decided I ought to leave it up to you. I'd like to ask you if you have any objection or reluctance about you and I getting together on a professional basis. Do you think you can try that?"

"I suppose so," John said.

As you can guess, John easily got appointments with all three of the first three people he approached in this manner. And even though he gave "tip-toe-on-ice" sales presentations, two of the three immediately became clients, and one referred several friends. Word spread and soon some members of the organizations he belonged to were actually seeking him out and asking him questions about his services.

Do you have a "discomfort" robbing you of happiness in selling? Face up to it. Acknowledge it. Devise a strategy to relieve it.

Realize that happiness and peace of mind are not "things" you find somewhere outside of yourself or that can be provided to you (or taken away from you) by others. Happiness and peace of mind are not "destinations" you get to "someday." Happiness and peace of mind are products of a healthy, goal-directed, proud self-image.

Chapter 8

How to Enjoy Financial Success in a Life of Professional Selling

Whatever the majority of people is doing, under any given circumstances, if you do the exact opposite, you will probably never make another mistake as long as you live. —Earl Nightingale

Yes, I know we talked about ways you can quickly and significantly increase your income in selling in the previous chapter as well as throughout all the chapters. But a high income does not always mean financial success. I have seen peers of mine, doctors; executives and entrepreneurs; and super successful sales professionals earn incomes in excess of $100,000 a year, year after year, still with little to show for it and still running ever-faster after the next desperately needed dollar. How can this be?

I do not pretend to be a financial genius, but you cannot be as serious a student of human behavior as I am without also studiously observing how people deal with the money that flows into and *through* their fingers in their lifetimes. In doing so, I have noted the few habits that rob even the highest money earners of financial security and independence, and I have formulated my beliefs about why these habits are so prevalent.

First, let me share a secret that I was very fortunate to learn at a relatively young age. Understanding this secret empowered me to make certain that my opportunities to earn large incomes did not go to waste; that I was able to use it to create financial independence for my wife and I, so that we enjoyed many years late in life absolutely free of any money worries or sacrifices. I say "secret" because so few people seem to understand this truth that it might as well be the closely and selfishly guarded secret of a small, elite, wealthy class. It's not, but it might as well be. It is this: that a high income is almost irrelevant if it is not used to create equity. The difference between income and equity is all important.

Income is here today, gone tomorrow. Most sales professionals who leap up to high earnings spend their incomes quickly and foolishly. Often they buy things that lose rather than gain value over time, like fancy cars, boats, overbuilt and overpriced homes, gaudy jewelry. Sometimes they blow sizeable sums in bars and nightclubs, generously paying for round after round, showing off. All too often, the commission check from the big sale disappears thanks to "wine, women and song," with little left to prove it was ever collected, except perhaps a grand hangover and an income tax liability.

I'm not opposed to living well. I've made a point of living well myself. In fact, if you do not reward yourself as well as your family for your hard work and extra efforts, you'll soon lose your "spark." As the saying goes, all work and no play makes Jack a dull boy.

But you do not want to have hundreds of thousands of dollars slip through your fingers only to wake up after five, ten, or more years with a pile of lifestyle debt to service, an urgent need for that next commission check, still having to perform to pay bills, still working because you must rather than by choice. This is why equity or net worth is so much more important than income. You can increase your income year after year and still be broke. But you cannot increase net worth year after year and be broke. The most important question to ask is not "am I making more money this year than last?," but "is my net worth greater this year than last?"

By the way, the use of income to create financial stability is so important because failing to do so ultimately sets a vicious cycle of self-image destruction in motion. The person who works hard and earns an exceptional income yet never seems to get ahead and is always living paycheck to paycheck eventually begins to question everything about his/her life, selling career and judgement. Financial pressures can shrink one's self-image to the size of a small potato. On the other hand, prosperity and a feeling of prosperousness and independence feeds on itself and strengthens the self-image. For maximum mental health, you must give your self-image the edge of measurable, meaningful progress toward financial security as opposed to just filling one pocket only to empty it just as quickly, then racing to fill it again.

Here are the habits I have taken note of, that determine whether high income leads to financial independence or financial frustration.

Spending vs. Investing

There is a very simple discipline that will serve you well: decide on a set percentage of all the income that comes to you that is taken off the top and put into secure investments certain to gain in value over time. It might be 1%, it might be 10%; pick a percentage you can live with and stick to it.

If you spend your income, you cannot gain equity from year to year. The best way to be certain you do not spend all your income is to take some off the top and invest that before you spend even a cent.

A warning: do *not* wait to begin cultivating this habit until you have "extra money" or until this, that, or the other thing occurs. Begin *immediately*, even if you have unpaid bills and believe you cannot afford to begin. Do it anyway. Do it now. Nothing will better convince the self-image that you are a prosperous person certain to attract plenty of opportunity, good fortune and money than seeing you make frequent deposits into your investment account.

Spending to Impress Others vs. Spending to Satisfy Yourself

Many people get themselves into serious financial trouble by spending their incomes trying to impress colleagues, neighbors, clients or girlfriends or boyfriends. In many salesforces, a one-upmanship culture takes hold, so as soon as one salesperson buys a new car, the others feel an urgent compulsion to buy new cars too. At annual meetings and conferences, each salesman's wife must be decked out in more expensive clothes and jewelry than the next, the saleswomen's husbands in costly custom suits and Rolex watches. If you have paid attention to everything else I've written in this book and in *Psycho-Cybernetics*, you can diagnose the seeds of this behavior easily. This is a frail, unconfident self-image trying to buy respect and approval. But this is futile, because gaining the respect of others requires self-respect.

Again, I have nothing bad to say about spending some of your money for personal pleasure. If a night on the town including limousine and driver, fanciest supper club, and theater is enjoyable, by all means, enjoy! You do not need my permission or anyone else's permission or my approval or anyone else's approval to spend the money you earn as you choose. The important words are "as *you* choose."

Choice is a very interesting thing. We humans are gifted with free will. Yet we so often abdicate it to others, by seeking their approval, their admiration, even their envy when self-approval and self-respect are the only paths to genuine happiness and peace of mind.

A man I know who, today, owns millions of dollars of real estate in several major cities, says he began while still a college student, working his way through school without benefit of scholarship, grant, or parental support. He bought his first piece of real estate, raw land that ultimately proved worthless, on an installment contract requiring payment of just $9 a month. To pay that $9, he had to suffer the taunts and derision of classmates who urged him to go out on the town, go to a local bar and have a few beers, and so forth; he had to decline, in order to save the money to make his monthly payment. To pay that $9, he had to sacrifice peer approval. He wore old, unfashionable clothes. He avoided the Thursday night poker games at the dorm. He made choices that were unpopular, viewed as weird, as too "straight" by those around him he desperately wished to have as friends. He now says that first piece of land was the worst real-estate investment of his entire life, but the very best investment in personal character-building he's ever made.

Deficit Spending vs. Living Within Your Means

Our national government has gotten all of us, our children and our grandchildren into a terrible mess thanks to its cheerful willingness to indulge in a continuing orgy of deficit spending. By spending money it does not have and only hopes to receive in the future, the federal government has accumulated such a sizeable debt it can never be paid off. Just servicing the interest on this debt is choking our economy, endangering the health and safety of our population, allowing our infrastructure of highways and transportation systems to deteriorate, and obligating future generations to financial slavery. You undoubtedly share my abhorrence for and anger at this irresponsible behavior on the part of our elected officials. Yet, do you tolerate or excuse the same irresponsible behavior in yourself?

As a side note, it is quite common to sharply criticize others for traits of our own we are guilty about or ashamed of. It is much tougher to look myself in the mirror and say, "Maxie, you wouldn't want to have to defend that, would you?" than to turn your back to the mirror and waggle a finger at someone else.

Deficit spending has become enormously popular in America. The idea of "saving up" to buy a new washer, dryer or refrigerator, new coat or outfit, or for a vacation is looked on as hopelessly old-fashioned. Modern society offers instant gratification with credit. The popularization of credit cards turned almost all Americans into debtors. The temptation to live beyond one's income is considerable. And many high-income sales professionals succumb, living significantly beyond their income, buying things with credit to be paid for later with anticipated, future earnings. This habit makes one a slave rather than a master, and severely weakens and undermines the health and vitality of the self-image.

The interest paid on consumer debt is an insidious cancer that eats away the net worth of even high-income earners. When interest effectively doubles, triples or quadruples the total price paid for all sorts of goods and services, no ordinary mortal can out-earn the damage.

The sales world is full of people earning $100,000 to $150,000 a year who are literally enslaved to the issuers of credit.

Eventually, this takes its toll. The person is surrounded by expensive luxury, material goods, and a lifestyle that impresses those not privy to his/her true financial condition. But he/she is increasingly frustrated and unhappy, realizing how little independence or security there is, living commission check to commission check even after years of earning an excellent income. Instead of viewing the future with optimism the person fears it. He/she worries that a slump, an illness, some sudden adverse turn of events will topple his/her "house of cards." The person worries that the people he/she has tried to impress will somehow perceive that "the emperor has no clothes." Sometimes this person even finds him- or herself desperate for the next sale; yet desperate salespeople cannot sell. The pressure of debt may even derail the career entirely. I'll tell you about such a person in a few minutes.

The greatest favor a high-income earner can do for him- or herself is to get out of debt and then to stay out of debt. In our modern society, you just about have to carry and use credit cards, especially to travel and entertain. But these should be paid off every month, not in so-called minimum monthly payments. Major purchases should be saved for, not bought now and paid for later. This admittedly unusual approach can totally free you from all money pressure. As a medical doctor, I will even say that such financial freedom and its associated freedom from frustration, worry, and stress is quite likely to extend your life span by years, reduce your risk of many debilitating diseases including cancer, and add quality to your life.

Greg Stanley, the President of a Phoenix, Arizona-based company, Whitehall Management, has coached and counseled literally thousands of doctors of chiropractic, dentistry and other disciplines to the successful achievement of financial independence and security. Greg Stanley's seminars and "boot camps" are legendary in these professions. And a cornerstone of Greg Stanley's teachings for these high-income professionals is the eradication of consumer debt from their lives. I suggest to you that what's good financial medicine for the doctors is good medicine for you, too.

Why Do So Many People Misuse Money?

I want you to meet a man I had a very in-depth dialogue with, about his financial habits and problems—a very successful sales representative for a major national company. We'll call him Elliott.

ELLIOTT: Dr. Maltz, I'm very disturbed about my finances.

MM: What's the problem?

ELLIOTT: I make a very good income and have for a number of years, but I don't have much to show for it. People who make less than I do are always talking about their investments and I don't have any. We're renting our home. I always seem to need all my commissions just to pay my bills. I'm worried about what will happen years from now, when I can't sell anymore or I want to retire.

MM: Well, Elliott, I'm no finance expert, and you probably ought to get some help from a credit counselor or financial planner.

ELLIOTT: Maybe, but I think my problems are psychological.

MM: What makes you say that?

ELLIOTT: I got to thinking about it last week, after I heard your lecture. My Dad has sort of a low opinion of what I do. He never directly says so, but he often makes disparaging remarks about salespeople he's dealt with, calls them sharks, and complains about how hard he and the other guys in the factory work for their wages while the salesmen stand around and drink coffee, go to fancy lunches, and make too much money too easily for their own good.

MM: That's a mouthful all right. But what do you believe about salespeople in general and about what you do?

ELLIOTT: I know that what salespeople do is important and useful. You know, nothing happens until somebody sells something and all that. But there are a lot of people like Dad who work a whole lot harder for their wages than I work. It doesn't seem fair, does it?

MM: Maybe, maybe not. Let's go back to your money. What do you do to save money? To invest for the future?

ELLIOTT: Truthfully nothing. I've tried. I've opened savings accounts, but wound up closing them after I raided them for one reason or another. I hate the very idea of living on a budget.

MM: It's pretty clear you aren't going to accumulate any money that way. There are any number of little gimmicks we could use to fix that, but if you're right, and you are washing your hands of money as rapidly as it comes to you because of some psychological monkey business, no gimmick's going to work.

ELLIOTT: That's what I'm afraid of.

MM: You know, if I operate on a patient and do surgery that restores a man's face after an accident or maybe enhances the beauty of a young woman, I might make as much in two hours as you make all month. Is that unfair?

ELLIOTT: It's no secret that doctors make a lot of money. But you did go to school for years, you spent a lot of money doing that—a doctor like you—a specialist, has a lot of skill that's relatively rare. I guess you're entitled.

MM: Nice of you. But what about a top salesman? He not only went to school but he's constantly going to seminars and training classes, studying books, learning to use computers. He invests a lot of money in keeping his skills sharp. He has to dress well, so he invests a bit of money in suits and ties. He has to keep an automobile in good working order and looking good. And he certainly has skills that are relatively rare—the top sales professional probably knows as much about human nature and human behavior as most psychologists, psychiatrists or counselors. He/she has to learn how to ask diagnostic questions, present information in an organized and interesting way, and to handle disappointment and frustration.

ELLIOTT: Put like that, there's a lot to this selling business.

MM: So let's say that a top sales pro makes a lot more money than, say, a fellow who pumps gas in a service station, an auto mechanic, or even a factory worker, is that fair or unfair?

ELLIOTT: I'm not sure.

MM: Look, I know it's difficult to talk about your father or mother objectively, but let's try for just a minute or two. Doesn't a factory worker have opportunities? Couldn't a factory worker go to night school and acquire skills that would lead to a better paying job? Couldn't a factory worker start a business on the side to increase income? Could a factory worker even learn to sell and become a salesman?

ELLIOTT: I guess so, but . . .

MM: Yes, everybody's closet of excuses is full of "but's." But there's nothing really stopping anybody from getting ahead in America. Deep down inside, the factory worker knows that. Today he/she's unhappy with the sum total of available choices. So he/she's resentful and jealous of others who have an easier time of it. The factory worker tries to make him- or herself feel better by making anybody like that within earshot feel bad. And may not do that consciously, but that's how his/her damaged and weak self-image struggles to make the worker feel better.

ELLIOTT: That's disturbing.

MM: If you are guilty about your money, then your money is making you unhappy. You don't want to feel that way. Just like the factory worker, you instruct your Servo-Mechanism to make you feel better. The factory worker's Servo-Mechanism obeys by demeaning other people. Your Servo-Mechanism obeys by taking your money away from you.

ELLIOTT: At that rate, I'll be commission check to commission check for the rest of my life.

MM: Could be. But let's experiment with a few things, just to see what happens.

ELLIOTT: No harm done.

MM: Okay, here's my prescription for you. First, the gimmick. You're going to open up a savings account at a bank in a distant city, at least 1,000 miles away, so it will be a difficult task to go there and make a withdrawal. Then every Friday you're going to send a deposit there equal to 10% of all the money you make during the week.

ELLIOTT: I'm barely making it. I can't take a 10% pay cut.

MM: We'll see.

ELLIOTT: All right, although I can't see the point.

MM: Hopefully you will. Now, second, I want you to devote a full hour every day to sitting in a comfortable chair, in a quite place, eyes closed, creating little mental movies of what it would be like if you were financially secure. Put together a movie of a mortgage-burning party, when your house is paid for. Another about your meeting with your stock broker and financial advisor. And so on.

ELLIOTT: Seems a little goofy.

MM: Uh-huh. Now, finally, I want you to read the sort of thing people of wealth read. Read *The Wall Street Journal* every day. Read magazines like *Money, Personal Finance*, even *Fortune*.

ELLIOTT: Then what?

MM: Let's get together again in three months.

The Wealth Rejection Syndrome, a Disease of the Self-Image

I have come to the conclusion that a person's attitudes about money are far more significant than his/her investing aptitudes, and certainly far, far more significant than luck or good fortune, in determining his/her wealth, security and financial success over time.

Many top earners, like Elliott, suffer from what I now call *wealth rejection syndrome*. It is a disease of the self-image. Its chief causes are guilt, extreme religious indoctrination, hypnosis in upbringing, and peer pressure.

Guilt about how you make your money, how easily you make your money, or how much money you make can instruct your Servo-Mechanism to get rid of it as fast as you get it. You can hear that in Elliott's story.

Extreme religious indoctrination has made many people devoutly believe that wealth is evil and poverty is good. This is so patently ridiculous it's a wonder to me that it sticks with anybody. But it does. Let me tell you why this is off base, both spiritually and as a practical matter. I will argue that God created abundance all around us and placed absolutely no limits on how much of that abundance we enjoy and benefit from. We limit ourselves, of course, in all sorts of ways: ignorance, stupidity, laziness, lack of discipline, superstition, and so on. But God placed no such limitations on us nor any limitations on how much of all the goodness of life we are to experience.

As a practical matter, anyone who insists that money or wealth is evil must desire to return to living in caves, killing wild animals with sticks for food, and grunting at each other as our only means of communication, because all progress since then has required the use of money as well as the creation and reinvestment of wealth. The scholarships that enable a student to go to college and to medical school; the hospital in which he or she will operate; the telephone lines through which a child will make a 911 emergency call when her father topples over in front of her with a heart attack; the ambulance that will get him to the hospital in time for his life to be saved; all these things are the result of wealth created and wealth reinvested. Rather than being the root of all evil, money, wealth creation and wealth reinvestment is the natural, vibrant juice of all human progress.

By "hypnosis in upbringing," I mean that a great many people are so thoroughly, consistently and ardently indoctrinated by parents, other family members, teachers and other authority figures in an antiwealth attitude that they are, in effect, hypnotized to avoid wealth, and reject it. Consider the simple phrase *filthy rich*. How many times have you heard it? Do you want to be a "filthy" person? Of course not. All too often, people, parents of limited means and limited opportunities unload all their disappointment, frustration, envy and resentment about their lot in life on their children. Instead of telling the children that they can be great, can excel, and that they can, in fact, grow rich if they desire, and instead of educating them in the fundamental truths of our free enterprise system—namely, that wealth is most often a representation of service and discipline—they admonish their children against expecting too much from life, tell them that the rich are evil, and literally hypnotize them against success.

Finally, there is peer pressure. Negative peer pressure can infect a healthy self-image and, over time, cancerize it, or negative peer pressure can easily reinforce an already negative self-image. Association with people who are constantly belittling you and your ambitions, constantly whining about how they are unfairly treated by life and insisting that you are and will be too can only lead you in one unhappy direction. Such people are expressing their own badly damaged self-images. They are telling you the truth as they see it, viewed through unsuccessful life experiences. The saying "misery loves company" tells this story.

Any one or combination of these influences can convince your self-image that you are just not meant to be rich. Convinced that this is so, the self-image instructs your superpowerful Servo-Mechanism to make absolutely certain that, under no conditions or circumstances, are you to keep much of the money you earn, successfully save and invest it, or otherwise develop financial security and independence. And it will do just that.

A Look at the Wealth Rejection Syndrome at Work

Are lottery winners cursed? If you look at the outcomes, you might think so. After winning two million dollars in a California lottery, Brett Peterson, a busboy in a restaurant, went on a wild spending spree, ran up his credit cards to the max, indiscriminately loaned thousands of dollars to friends, and "partied" until he was broke. Just months after getting his first lottery check, Brett Peterson had to get a lowest-rung-on-the-ladder sales clerk job just to make ends meet, keep roof overhead, and beans on the table.

Lynette Nichols, a six-dollar-an-hour bookkeeper, was one of three winners of a giant forty-eight million dollar lottery jackpot in Texas. But she'd barely gotten winnings in hand when she and her husband started fighting—over money! She objected to his wasting money on expensive electronic gadgets for himself. He objected to her lavishing cars and other expensive gifts on her side of the family. The two wound up in a bitter divorce that cost each of them hundreds of thousands of dollars and turned the winning of the lottery into the destruction of a marriage. (Incidentally, if you assume her winnings to be roughly eight or nine million dollars after taxes, probably paid out over time, perhaps equating to $700,000 a year, you have to ask yourself: at what price a marriage?)

Charles Rice Jr. won sixteen million dollars in a lottery, but quickly had the new Corvette sports car he bought with winnings impounded after he allegedly used it to assault two police officers. The injured police officers each sued him for a million dollars. Pat McKenna, a New York construction worker, won seven million dollars, but he cannot enjoy it; immediately afterward, he was arrested and jailed for drunk driving.

These kinds of stories about the curse of the lottery jackpot are not at all uncommon. Why would so many lottery winners experience so much tragedy, suffering, and chaos in their lives?

One explanation may be what I call the *self-image snap back effect*. Think of the self-image as a thick rubber band. You can stretch it quite a bit beyond its oval shape and you can forcibly hold it out there, but the second you cease your active stretching, the rubber band snaps right back to its original form, sometimes weaker than it was before. The person who gets sudden, unearned wealth dumped in his/her lap and doesn't have the self-image prepared for it seems very likely to shift into self-sabotage almost overnight. Similarly, the sales pro who enjoys rapid, substantial income increases is stretching the rubber band, but at some point, can't stretch anymore and it snaps back. You simply cannot sustain any success that is outside the acceptance range of your self-image. And if you do achieve such success, the self-image rears up and says "Wait just a minute there, buster. What makes you think you deserve 'x'? Why, nobody in your whole family ever got anywhere close to 'x'! You certainly don't have enough education/experience/talent/know-how/good looks/whatever for 'x'. Get back where you belong." Snap.

Keep in mind that the self-image must be conditioned, strengthened and prepared for the success you seek.

Back to Elliott's story. Yes, he returned for a visit after two months. I frankly wouldn't say that the transformation was remarkable, but it was a beginning. Elliott was discovering new answers.

"Dr. Maltz," he said, "the bank account gimmick is interesting. I've sent that money in every Friday just like you said. It's a funny thing, but I haven't missed it much. I'm still in about the same place with my bills. I haven't had to eat beans or anything like that. But I've got over $700 in that darned bank account. What's more interesting is that I've started to look forward to mailing in those deposits, and I feel good after I do it. I feel like I'm accomplishing something. I'm reading *The Wall Street Journal* and those other magazines, and for the first time in my life, getting interested in making money work for me. But the strangest thing is, my income's going up. I'm closing more sales, but I don't think I'm doing anything differently. Why do you think that is?"

"You may not be doing anything differently," I said, "but you are beginning to think differently."

My Prescriptions for Your Financial Health and Well-Being

1. Scale down your expenses so you are living within your income, with money left over. Nothing other than this is acceptable.

2. Set up a plan and timetable to get out of debt. Commit to the goal of debt-free living.

3. Set and achieve financial and material goals of your own making, don't play "keep up with the Joneses."

4. Start saving, investing if possible. At the very least, open a "wealth-building account" and put a set percentage of every dollar that comes to you into that account, without fail.

5. Begin building the healthy self-image of a person who not only earns an exceptional income but is also a good steward of the good fortune that comes his or her way.

Chapter 9

The Zero-Resistance Experience: Eight Steps to Creating Your Own Zero-Resistance Selling Experience

You get up in the morning, awakened by your own mental alarm clock. You have had a good, peaceful night's sleep and awaken refreshed and alert, eager to get going. As you shower, shave, and dress, you run through your affirmations, your schedule for the day, and anticipate specific results you will achieve from the day's planned activities. You enjoy a pleasant breakfast with your spouse and children. On the way to your first meeting of the day, you listen to an interesting, uplifting audiocassette tape. On arrival, before going in, you sit quietly in your parked car, close your eyes, and briefly visit the Theater of Your Mind, where you recall the winning feeling you experienced when successfully completing a negotiation very similar to the one you are about to begin. Still in the theater, you also quickly rerun the Mental Rehearsal movie you've made of the upcoming meeting. Relaxed and confident, you enter the meeting. No surprise to you, it is mostly deja vu, just as you rehearsed. When the meeting is completed, you place the signed contracts in your briefcase, shake hands all around, and walk to your car, noting with a smile that the entire negotiation was completed with very little resistance to your ideas and suggestions—and what little resistance was offered, you cut through like a heated butter knife effortlessly slicing through a cold, hard stick of butter!

Why shouldn't you have this kind of selling experience everyday? The keys follow:

Step One: Use Your Imagination

Walt Disney used his imagination to create wonderful worlds that bring joy, happiness and wonder to millions of children and adults alike, invigorate the cities in which they are based, and create a legacy that continues living, thriving, and growing long after his passing.

Lee Iacocca used his imagination to see opportunity where everyone else saw crisis, to envision success when everyone else saw impending disaster, to turn a virtually bankrupt corporation into a fantastic success.

Conrad Hilton, creator of the famous Hilton hotel chain, often talked about the times he spent opening and operating grand hotels in his imagination. Mr. Hilton said that he imagined himself to be a successful hotel man and that he felt like a successful hotel man long before he became one.

As a plastic surgeon, I used my imagination to create very detailed, precise mental movies of the operations I performed before I performed them, so that each actual operation was deja vu.

You can use your imagination to create a selling career you can be proud of and happy with. You can use your imagination to create a zero-resistance selling experience. You can use the "synthetic experience" of imagined events to set up actual events so that they are deja vu.

Everything happens first in the imagination. In this book, I've shown you many different ways to work through your own imagination, to activate your Automatic Success Mechanism. You should use these methods every day of your life.

Why is it so important to deliberately, strategically use the imagination? Let me tell you about a great psychological secret that governs success and failure, exhilaration and frustration in our lives.

Once when I was speaking to a group of executives, a boy of 14, Ray, was there to blow his bugle, to play "Yankee Doodle Dandy" in my honor. But when he raised the instrument to his mouth on cue, nothing happened. Try as he might, his face blue with the effort, Ray could not blow his horn. When I got up to speak, I said "The topic of my talk today is Ray, Who Couldn't Blow

His Horn." I went on to say that there are many Rays in our midst who, because of some fear or anxiety manufactured in their own imaginations, cannot blow their horns. If your imagination is undirected, left to wander around on its own, it will, more often than not, manufacture images that promote anxiety and fear. This is what sabotages so many people in sales, as well as in other fields. You *must* control your imagination! You must demand that it work for you, not against you, and direct it to support you, not undermine you. This is up to you!

Stop taking your awesomely powerful imagination for granted. Stop letting it wander around and make trouble, without supervision. Everyday, make deliberate use of your imagination to achieve your potential.

Step Two: Strengthen Your Self-Image

I hope I have succeeded in stimulating your fascination with the self-image, so that you will become a dedicated and determined student of it, and that you will do everything you can to strengthen your own self-image. When the self-image is healthy and strong, you have pride, self-confidence, the ability to express yourself effectively, and a glow or aura about you that magnetically attracts cheerful cooperation, acceptance and trust, and melts resistance as easily as a heated butter knife slicing through a stick of butter! When the self-image is sickly and weak and vulnerable, you feel anxious, and inferior, hide rather than express yourself, easily accept resistance and are tossed about on the waves of life's ocean like a ship without a rudder.

The greatest news of our generations has been that the self-image can be changed by choice and conscious effort. You are not, in any way whatsoever, stuck with the programming that may be in there at this moment.

Let's assume that you join an adult tag-football league, and you want to play well. If you are intelligent about that goal, you will begin doing things to get into better physical shape. You will modify your diet. You will exercise daily. You may use a treadmill, to build up your endurance. Lift weights, to create better upper-body strength. Nobody questions this at all. Everybody understands that a person can change his/her physical strength, stamina and performance by altering diet and utilizing exercise.

It is exactly the same with your goals to excel in selling. If you are smart about these goals, you will begin doing things to get into better mental and emotional shape. You will modify your mental diet. You will use self-image strengthening exercises daily. Go back through this book and the exercises provided immediately after this chapter, and put together your own daily self-image fitness program.

Step Three: Use Mental Rehearsal

The famous basketball coach John Wooden said: "Unless a kid can clearly visualize the basketball going through the basket, there's no chance he can throw it in when he has to."

In my book *Psycho-Cybernetics* I describe how a number of top pro golfers rely on a step-by-step system for first making each golf shot inside their imaginations. When the great golfer Ben Hogan was playing tournament golf regularly, he kept a golf club in his bedroom and often practiced in private, swinging the club correctly and without pressure at an imaginary golf ball. When he was actually on the links, he would go through the correct motions in his imagination before making a shot.

There *is* a very direct connection between Mental Rehearsal and real experience. While it takes time, patience and creative imagination to mentally rehearse, the pay-off can be dramatic. One of the leading members of the Million Dollar Roundtable in the insurance industry in 1961, the year after I wrote *Psycho-Cybernetics*, told me that his success at closing sales to new prospects more than doubled once he adhered to the rule of mentally rehearsing each meeting before it occurred. You can make resistance from prospects disappear by first erasing it in Mental Rehearsal.

I was once the guest of a coach at a football game, and got to sit on the bench with the players and be in the locker room before and after the game. In the third quarter, losing by two touchdowns, the first-string quarterback was injured and came out of the game. The second-string quarterback was already injured. So in went the third string quarterback, who had never played a minute of pro ball yet in his life, and had never even practiced with the first string squad. On third down and twenty some odd yards to go, the "green" quarterback threw a perfect pass forty yards down the field. It landed right in the receiver's hands, held out in front of him, as he streaked down the sideline. A touchdown! Afterward I asked the young player how he was able to throw that pass so confidently and perfectly, while under so much pressure, never having practiced with that center, that offensive line or that receiver before. "Dr. Maltz, I've thrown that exact pass to that receiver 1,000 times in my imagination."

Do you have the discipline and commitment to mentally rehearse the perfect sales presentation 1,000 times?

Step Four: Use Affirmations

I talk to myself all the time and you do too. Most people never give this much thought, and the "inner dialogue" they carry on with themselves just happens. But it's this continuing conversation that programs the Servo-Mechanism! You *must* pay attention to what you are telling your Servo-Mechanism. Be alert for unproductive inner talk, like "if it wasn't for bad luck, I wouldn't have any luck at all". . .or "a day late and a dollar short, that's just the way I am". . . or "I've never been able to sell to this kind of a tough prospect—I guess today won't be any different." And so on. What terrible things to tell your Servo-Mechanism!

Go into the kitchen, pour yourself a tall glass of cool water. But before you take that first satisfying swallow, take some rat poison and dump it in. Would you do that? Of course not. So why poison your own mind? Why continue recycling the same poisonous statements through your imagination over and over again?

Beyond that, you *can* reprogram the Servo-Mechanism and strengthen the self-image by deliberately creating and frequently repeating statements that affirm your best qualities, past successes, and worthy ambitions. What kind of person are you? You are the kind of person you create in the self-image, and affirmations are a powerful tool.

The Dallas Cowboys' Super Bowl quarterback Troy Aikman says that the Knute Rockne-type pep talk delivered in the locker room by a fire-breathing coach is pretty much a thing of the past. "We are highly paid, intelligent, goal-oriented professionals," he said, "and we are expected to get ourselves motivated, to go out and perform at our best." If you want to be a highly paid, peak performance professional, you should understand this. You cannot wait for anyone else to "motivate" you. You must create self-motivation with tools like affirmations.

Step Five: Use Psychological Triggers

Think of *psychological triggers* as visual affirmations, as instant reminders of your "big self." I urge people to write their affirmations or just key words like *confidence, big potato,* and *abundance* on 3 x 5 inch file cards and tack them up at their desks, put them on the bathroom mirror, or the refrigerator door. Get a large potato from the grocery store and put it on your desk, to trigger thoughts of strengthening your self-image to grow to the size of a giant potato, rather than shrinking to the size of a small potato.

I know a doctor who hates completing the forms he has to send to the insurance companies for payment. These pile up on his desk unattended to for weeks. His staff nagged to no avail. At my suggestion, he has his assistant staple a photocopy of a $100 bill to each form he must fill out. This visual reminder that each completed form equals money in the bank helps him to dig into this work.

Have fun and experiment with different ways that you can stimulate your powerful Servo-Mechanism into productive action.

Step Six: Stop—Think—Choose

Throughout this book, I've talked to you about choices. You really do *choose* to sell against resistance—or be free of it! How do you make that choice? *It is the sum total of hundreds of little choices you make,* from the moment you get out of bed in the morning, look your mug in the mirror and say"Hey Charlie—what kind of day am I going to make this today?" until you lie down in bed at night. These little choices have a cumulative impact that literally controls the results you experience in selling, and in life.

You choose your thoughts. When a thought enters your consciousness, you must *Stop!—Think*: what good is this doing me? Is this productive? Will this contribute to my success? Is it accurate? What voice is speaking here, my harshest Critic Within or my coach-with-kind-eyes? What direction will this point my Servo-Mechanism in? Will this activate my ASM or my AFM?

You choose your emotions. When an emotion wells up from inside, to take control of your actions, you must *Stop!—Think*: is this my "big self" or "little self"? Is this fear, frustration, anger or resentment? *Or* is it confidence, creativity, compassion? Is this an emotion to be ashamed of or proud of? Is this enhancing or dissipating my energy?

You choose your actions. As you invest your precious time during the day, every once in a while you must *Stop!—Think*: is this habit or creative? Is this contributing to reaching my goals or distracting me from them? Is this important or trivial? Stop—Think—Choose!

Step Seven: Use Your Down Time to Recharge for the Next Day

John D. Rockefeller said that he ended each day by slowly and methodically emptying his pockets. As he took things out of his pockets, he made a conscious effort to empty his mind of all worry, anxiety, and frustration. This is a wonderful example of a Psycho-Cybernetic technique for relaxation.

You need relaxation for renewal. At the end of the day, you should defuse your frustration, celebrate thanksgiving for the opportunities and accomplishments of the day, and relax. Please don't do this with chemicals. The do-it-yourself tranquilizers available free of charge right in your own imagination are safer, more powerful and more beneficial than any pills you can buy in the pharmacy or alcoholic beverage you might consume.

If you present yourself to the world feeling tired, fatigued, frustrated, stressed or insecure, you invite resistance. Prospects, clients, and customers "feel" your own uncertainty and insecurity. It transfers to them. It undermines trust and makes decision-making impossible. But when you present yourself to the world relaxed, renewed, and confident, your prospects, clients or customers "feel" that security. It enhances trust and makes decision-making comfortable.

During the last days of World War II someone commented to President Harry Truman that he appeared to bear up under the stress and strain of the presidency better than any previous President; that the job did not appear to have aged him or sapped his vitality, and that this was remarkable, especially in view of the many problems which he faced as a war-time president. His answer was: "I have a foxhole in my mind." President Truman meant that he was able to go inside his own imagination, escape stress, and relax. Everybody should have a foxhole in their own minds!

I urge people to create their own personal "quiet place" in their imaginations, in copious detail. If you find the ocean or a quiet lake particularly relaxing, by all means build a luxurious beach-front vacation home, with thatched roof, lazily turning ceiling fans, comfortable furniture, and a porch that directly faces the ocean, where you can sit, favorite beverage in hand, and watch sailboats go by. If you find the woods more to your liking, build yourself a mountain lodge out of rock and timber, surrounded by tall shade trees, next to a babbling brook. With a bit of practice, you'll be able to close your eyes and instantly transport yourself to your quiet place and mentally "shift" into decompression and relaxation. This is a terrific thing to do at the end of the day, so you do not carry any of your hard-to-forget business troubles into your home. This is a very useful thing to do before going into an important business meeting, so you can "clear the calculator" and go into the meeting relaxed, renewed, and focused.

Step Eight: Keep Your Eye on the Goal

Psycho-Cybernetics means the deliberate steering of all the powers of the human mind, in sync and in harmony, to a productive, rewarding goal. If you will stay focused on your goal, your Servo-Mechanism can be trusted to zig and zag as need be, to ultimately arrive at that goal just as surely as our military's most sophisticated guided-missile technology can be relied on to deliver the missile to its target.

What If You Want to Move Up the Corporate Ladder? Or Grow Your Own Company?

Unwrap your imagination! Mark Lipton, chair of human resources management and director of The Leadership Center, Milano Graduate School of Management and Urban Policy, cited a survey in the Sloan Management Review (Summer, 1996), of 1500 senior leaders, 870 CEOs from 20 different countries, which asked for the key traits CEOs would need for the year 2000. The number-one answer: the ability to convey a strong sense of vision. Lipton went on to lament that "more than 90% lack confidence in their ability to conceive of a vision."

It is widely believed that George Bush lost the 1992 Presidential election because of "this vision thing"—his inability to crystallize and convey a great vision for the future of the country and for the achievements that would take place in his second term. As this manuscript is being completed, candidate Bob Dole is having much the same problem. To many, his "vision" is focused on the past—a bit too "farsighted" for our needs today.

Leadership requires vision. Clear, confident, predictive vision. The ability not only to see things accurately as they are, to see things creatively as they can be, but also to creatively build the bridge between the two, and then to sell the entire vision to the world. In a very real sense, leadership is salesmanship practiced at a very high level. If you master Zero-Resistance selling, you also own Zero-Resistance leadership. So set your sights as high as you like!

Go into the Theater of Your Mind often, to keep constructing the vivid detail of the career and lifestyle you want to have. As it becomes clearer and clearer, you'll be closer and closer to attaining it. Sell yourself on your vision. Then begin selling others, to secure the cooperation you need.

The Ultimate Truth About All Resistance

We manufacture just about all the resistance we encounter.

Every thought you allow to linger, every habit you permit existence, every action you choose either magnifies or reduces resistance. That is the message of *Zero-Resistance Selling*: Sell yourself on it, apply it, and I know that you, too, will excel as a result.

Chapter 10

How to Use the Power of Networking to Enhance Your Zero-Resistance Selling Experience

If I had to name the single characteristic shared by all the truly success-ful people I've met over a lifetime, I'd say it's the ability to create and nurture a network of contacts. —Harvey Mackay

When frustrated and unsuccessful people complain about their lot in life, they often say that "it is not what you know but *who* you know that counts." and comment on how unfair this is. Hidden inside their misplaced frustration are clues for sales professionals striving for Zero-Resistance selling.

First of all, the whole idea of fair vs. unfair is something worthy of very little thought or attention. Resentment toward conditions you perceive as unfair can only sap your own energy. In order to succeed in life, you must learn how life works, and find ways to work with it. I can vividly recall all the things I noted in medical school that were terribly unfair. There was favoritism, nepotism, unreasonable demands, and abusive and dictatorial doctors who lorded their power over the students and interns. Impossibly long hours. Those of my peers who grew so frustrated and angry with this situation washed out. Those of us who found ways to cope, and, in some cases, turn the situation to our advantage, became doctors.

Let's just set aside the subject of fairness for the time being. With that done, we can acknowledge that "who you know" can be very important. In a great many cases, you'll never get the opportunity to demonstrate what you know without entre arranged for you by someone you know who knows the someone you need access to. This is the way of the world.

Further, if you focus on eliminating resistance, then the benefit of introductions multiplies in importance. Let's assume you sell certain investments and financial services, and wish to make a presentation to the president of a large company in your city. It will be very difficult to even get to this person "cold." But if you devise some combination of marketing strategies, maybe a series of clever letters, a "white paper" that interests him/her, and so on, you can probably persist and secure the desired appointment. And then you can go in and make your presentation. Contrast that with having someone that corporate president knows and respects calling him up or jotting him a note, introducing you and suggesting that you might have important information for him. In the first instance, where you get the appointment through your own efforts, when you begin your presentation, where will the level of resistance be? Very high. But in the second instance, where an introduction has been made for you, where will the level of resistance be? Very low.

This is why the most successful sales professionals I know have fat, bulging Rolodexes. Their network of contacts allows them to "pre-eliminate" resistance when they want to get to a certain person or certain type of person, as well as to do that favor for others.

I have gotten to know a great many super-successful people in my life, including sales professionals, executives, entrepreneurs, collegiate and pro coaches, literary agents and publishers, and, well, you name it, and if there is one thing they all have in common it is the fat, bulging Rolodex™.

I think the importance of networking is obvious. Yet most people do not do it at all, or if they do, they do it haphazardly and casually. Over the years, I've made a point of asking salespeople, doctors, accountants, and others if they actively work on their networks of useful contacts and, if not, why not.

The Three Reasons Why Salespeople Fail at Networking

The most common excuse for not networking is lack of time. But when people say "I don't have enough time," what do they really mean?

No one has enough time to do everything they need or want to do. Everyone makes choices, and finds the time to do some things while finding no time to do others. We all choose. We all prioritize. "I don't have enough time" is the excuse furnished by the Servo-Mechanism when you really don't want to do a particular thing. When you hear yourself say "I don't have enough time," you need to stop, go look in the mirror, and ask yourself for the real reasons why you wish to avoid doing that particular thing. After all, we should strive to use creative Psycho-Cybernetics to be truthful with ourselves. If you aren't going to tell yourself the truth, how will you have the courage to tell others truth or to hear truth from others? The truth can set you free, but not if you hide from it!

The first of the *real* reasons why people avoid networking is ego. As I've said before, unchecked, the hungry ego is a formidable enemy of success. There is such a profound difference between having a healthy self-image and an unhealthy ego! Egotistical people make lots of noise but really live in fear. So the egotist fears rejection to such a degree, he or she would rather never ask anything of anyone. This is crippling, because the exchanging of favors, in the case of networking, the exchanging of contacts and introductions, is what human commerce is all about. We create, build and strengthen friendships by exchanging favors. We build strong business relationships by exchanging favors. Not that you do it in a quid pro quo consciousness. I don't suggest that. But that you freely and cheerfully give information or contacts another person needs and can benefit from, certain in the knowledge that benefit will come back to you, and be willing to call on that person at some future time if he/she might be of help to you.

The person whose ego is determined to safeguard him/her from ever hearing the word "no" takes all the creative power away from the Servo-Mechanism almost as dramatically and completely as a big chunk of glowing green Kryptonite turns the comic book character Superman into a weakened mortal.

If the ego is not getting in the way with its damnable fear of rejection, it is interfering in another way—insisting that you ought to be above needing anyone's help. "I can make my own way in the world," one struggling, financially embarrassed salesperson once told me, indignantly, when I suggested she begin networking in earnest. "I don't need to be kissing up to other people left and right to get ahead. That's not how a real woman goes through life. Besides, my products and my proposition ought to stand on its own merits."

This woman has obviously had some rather limiting ideas ingrained in her self-image. She has a preconceived notion that networking is a degrading process. And her ego would never permit admitting the need for another's help. She probably never says "thank you" either.

The Secret Power Phrase That Removes Resistance Instantly

Ego deprives people of benefit from one of the most powerful resistance-melting techniques ever invented: asking for help.

One of the most powerful phrases in all of selling, in all of life, is "I wonder if you could help me with something. . . ." This phrase breaks down barriers and melts resistance like a heated butter knife. It turns icy, stiff and formal secretaries into warm, friendly conversationalists eager to give you all manner of information. It turns busy, high-and-mighty executives into unhurried conversationalists, happy to share their secrets of success, industry knowledge and contacts. Why does such a simple phrase have such a profound impact on people? In some cases, because it flatters their egos! In some cases, because it appeals to their good nature. A sincere, simple request for help is magic. But the person ruled by his/her own hungry ego can never utter this phrase. The person caught in the vice grip of an insatiable ego can never sincerely ask for help.

If you are now out of balance on the ego side, can you admit that to yourself, as a result of reading this book? If you can, then you can use the techniques of Psycho-Cybernetics to replace ego and fear with a healthy self-image and genuine self-confidence!

I'm Just Not Good at Meeting People

The second impediment to networking holding most people back is an acquired awkwardness for meeting new people. I notice that even a silver-tongued sales pro, confident and effective when selling in the environment he or she's used to, clams up and becomes a wallflower in search of a potted palm to hide behind, in a setting he/she's unfamiliar with. As an author and a speaker I've become very comfortable with meeting lots of new people, but I'll admit that they come up and introduce themselves to me, not vice versa. In my early days in practice, though, I made a point of getting out and about, to civic events and social events, to meet and befriend new people. I made a kind of a game out of seeing how many people I could meet and get to know in a day or an evening or at a particular event. I am very aware of how many people find this simple activity intimidating. If you are among them, you must understand that "shyness" is not genetic or natural or unchangeable. Because it is an instruction being given by the self-image to the Servo-Mechanism, it is very changeable.

Just as the ego can cause fear of rejection for some people, a weak and vulnerable self-image can cause the very same fear for others.

I remember talking to another doctor years ago about his reclusive nature. Although Rob was very well-to-do, and successful in practice, and we lived in the same neighborhood, we never saw him at medical association meetings, city activities, social affairs or local clubs. I once asked him if he made a point of building up his contacts, and he said that he did not; he avoided interaction with groups, and he and his wife kept to themselves.

MM: "Why do you choose to live like that?"

ROB: "I have no choice. If I go to any parties or gatherings, I do not dare answer others' questions about what I do. It's embarrassing to me and humiliating to my wife."

MM: "Good Lord, man, you're a doctor! How can that be humiliating?"

ROB: "Maybe you forget, Max, but I am a dentist."

MM: "So?"

ROB: "C'mon Max. Everybody hates dentists. As soon as I'm introduced as a dentist, somebody has to say he hates going to the dentist. And besides that, I know they all think I'm a dentist because I flunked out of medical school. Mary wants me to just say I'm a doctor and leave it at that. I'd prefer to avoid the confrontation altogether."

I wonder how many other people have similar hang-ups. Insurance salespeople, auto salespeople, waitresses, department store sales clerks, and on and on. When Psycho-Cybernetics was in its first heyday and just about everybody had heard about it, and I was introduced to a group of people as its author, there was almost always a wiseguy who would call it psychological mumbo-jumbo or ask how it felt to be a modern-day snake-oil salesman. I took my share of negativity first as a plastic surgeon, then later as the creator of this self-help information. I never let it drive me into fearful seclusion. In fact, I responded to it as a challenge, and sought ways to rise above it. I even occasionally got a bit sharp with people.

I vividly remember the first time I was ridiculed for being a plastic surgeon, in a circle of people, at a cocktail party. "So you cater to peoples' vanity, right doc?" the man said. "What price vanity?"

I thought about that and the next time a similar situation occurred, I quietly but firmly responded. I said, "Well, you are right that many people who have very trivial physical deformities but giant egos come to see me and sometimes I accommodate them. But what is more interesting, I think are, say, the burn victims, like the 9-year-old boy who lost half his face and had terrible scars all over his arms from a home fire. Restoring his good looks and self-esteem seems worthwhile to me. Now what is it you said you did for a living? As I recall, I drove one man away but made several new friends in that little conversation circle that evening!

Anyway, I sat down with my dentist friend and said, "Listen, you've magnified this negative attitude about dentists that some people have into a giant self-image-eating monster that is ruining your life. *You've* done this. Admittedly, Mary isn't helping, but she's really just reflecting back your own fears and insecurities. You became a dentist for good reason. You provide an important service. You do work you're proud of. But you can't blame people for saying they don't like going to the dentist. They've been conditioned to feel that way and even to say it. Let the truth set you free. Acknowledge that many people do have fears and negative feelings about dentists, and that's that. You need to be a confident and persuasive ambassador for dentistry, changing peoples' attitudes, not a coward hiding behind your couch with the blinds drawn. We can create some simple attitude-altering responses for you to use in conversation, as strategy, if you're willing to use them. I hope you will be. You're a professional deserving of respect and admiration. You must first decide that you will have the respect you deserve."

I'm delighted to tell you that my neighbor "saw the light" and began circulating. He has since, to my knowledge, joined a country club and became active in at least one nonprofit organization. He sent one member of his club, a marketing executive for a large sporting goods company, to me, and he hired me to speak at their convention. I referred an investment broker I've used for years to the dentist a few months ago; the broker had a new pension product I thought might interest the dentist. Networking.

Finally, there is one more reason some people avoid networking: guilt. These people focus on the quid pro quo aspect and say that they find it offensive. With probing, though, I usually find someone with a self-image that feels undeserving of others' respect and cooperation, undeserving of great success, and afraid they have little to offer and therefore have no right to ask and receive from others. You must understand that you and everyone else definitely has a great deal to offer to others around you.

Everyone brings something to the table. You have knowledge, experience, contacts that the businessperson across the street from you does not. And you can certainly take steps to strengthen your networking assets. If you have not given much thought to networking up until now, you probably have assets you are taking for granted, but that someone else might prize highly.

Getting Past "Quid Pro Quo"

I believe the universe itself rewards those who give—whether the giving be financial, a leg up, advice, reassurance, encouragement or a useful introduction—in multiples. You don't have to worry about getting a return on your gift directly from that particular recipient. You are guaranteed a generous return by certain universal, spiritual laws of life. As a practical matter, this does not mean you can suddenly give all your money to the poor and sit under a tree waiting to hit the lottery via divine intervention, nor does it mean you can give all your productive time away to any and all who will take it, and then expect money to fall from the sky over your head. One of the great challenges of life is to balance philosophy and practicality. While generosity is a virtue, sloth is a sin. So we must work smart and hard, and we must steward and use our resources wisely, so as to achieve meaningful goals. But generally speaking, frequently giving little bits of kindness, compassion, encouragement or even useful information to others takes little from you yet can bring abundant rewards to you.

Certainly if you do a favor for someone, you can reasonably expect a good response if and when you need to directly call on that same person for a favor. There is nothing wrong with that. There is nothing to feel guilty about in doing that. But you can rise far above that "tit for tat" approach and use networking in a much greater way.

The Man Who Brings Others Together

About ten years ago, after a lecture, I met a man who specifically asked I not identify him by name in my writings or talks. He is one of the richest and most successful entrepreneurs in America, up from very humble beginnings, in relatively few years. When I asked his secret of success, he said "I am the man who brings others together."

"What do you mean by that?" I asked.

"It's really very simple Dr. Maltz," he replied. "I've long made it a point not to focus on my businesses but instead to focus on everyone else's. I spend more time matchmaking than anything else. I have a client or an investor I don't know, just someone I meet like you, and I learn through conversation that this person owns diamond mines in Africa and is having considerable problems with the government over import tarrifs, or I learn that this person is an avid New York Yankees fan, or I learn that this person is of Greek heritage and longs to visit the Greek Islands but cannot afford to do so; then I may drop notes to him and another contact I have who is an expert in import/export, or I may get someone I know in the Yankees organization to send this fellow a ball autographed by one of the players, or I may have my travel agent, who happens to be Greek herself, and knows of many inexpensive ways to tour Greece to call this person. In this way, I put people together. This person with that person, that person with this person. Sometimes it involves something important, sometimes something trivial. I find that doing this, more than enough money comes my way." "How?" I asked.

"In so many different ways, I cannot count. A stock or investment tip here, a door opened there. You see, by placing myself in the center, with all these people and interests circling around me, and me causing them to pass me to meet each other, I become part of everything. I suppose people feel obligated, although I have never once directly asked for quid pro quo."

I gave this man an autographed copy of my book when we parted.

Yes, there's a more to this story. A few months later, I got a call from the CEO of a very large direct sales company, with over 30,000 dealers scattered all over the United States, Canada and Europe. He said he wanted to buy copies of my book *Psycho-Cybernetics* for all of his company's dealers, and wondered if I would come and speak at their national convention where the books were to be given out as gifts. When I asked how he had obtained the book and learned about me, he named this fellow—the man who brings others together.

"I mentioned to him in casual conversation that we were having difficulty keeping our sales troops motivated," the CEO said, "and a week later he sent me over a copy of your book and suggested I read it. I did and it is obviously what we need."

I sent "the man who brings others together" a nice thank-you note, and then for years, sent him the occasional card, postcard or news-clipping, and he did the same for me.

At one meeting I attended, I met a young man with a clever invention for the plumbing industry, but no money, and no idea how to go about getting his invention to market. I remembered that "the man who brings others together" also owned a hotel chain. I figured: he must know somebody in a big plumbing product company because of all the products bought for his hotels. So I sent the young inventor to him. He, in turn, got the young inventor to the right company, the product was a success, the young inventor grew rich, and "the man who brings others together" later sent me a thank-you note and a fine bottle of wine, mentioning that he had bought stock in the plumbing products company because of his confidence in this new product, and had done very well on his investment. It so happens that I had bought a bit of that stock too, at the suggestion of the young inventor.

"The man who brings others together" lives a simple principle often voiced by the famous motivational speaker Zig Ziglar: "You can get whatever you want in life if you help enough other people get what they want in life."

How This Consultant Becomes "The Talk of the Town" by Bringing Others Together

Somers White is a very interesting fellow. He is a former bank president, management consultant, consultant to speakers and authors, and a professional speaker. Almost every year, he is "the talk of the town" at the National Speakers Association Convention because of the by-invitation-only networking dinner he hosts.

A night or two before the convention, Somers hosts a formal, elegant dinner for 50 to 100 people. He invites past and present clients, peers, friends, and people with unusual expertise. He assigns the seating, so people meet each other—spouses do not even get to sit together! He even gets each person to stand up and he briefly interviews them about their businesses and interests. For every person at that dinner, he creates a Grade A+ networking opportunity.

As these people go out into the general population of the convention, they are all talking about this unusual event, and everybody who was not invited and included is curious about what went on there, and how they might get invited the next year. It is a brilliant strategy that many people could borrow and use in their own industries, professions or communities.

How to Be a Master Networker

These days, networking has become the trendy thing to do. Most cities have breakfast, lunch and cocktail hour "lead clubs," where businesspeople and sales professionals gather for the express purpose of networking.

Whether it's in such intentional settings or in other, less direct situations, there are a few characteristics that are shared by those deriving the greatest benefits from all this networking, and here they are:

First, a healthy self-image. Would you expect me to list anything else first? Of course not! Remember that your self-image absolutely controls your possibilities. If you see yourself as an outgoing, likeable, friendly person who easily meets others and who others are eager to talk to, then that is exactly the experience you will have.

If you want to get better at networking, you must pull together the evidence of your having a networking-oriented personality and use this to program your self-image for these desired results. Your self-image must be strong enough to shrug off occasional rejection, so that you can be free of fear.

Second, a genuine, keen interest in other people. What makes them tick? What do they know about that you know little about? People are, by far, the most interesting creatures on earth. Take 100 people and you can find 100 different backgrounds, 100 different fascinations, 100 different foibles.

Just as an aside, you want to avoid the "3 x 5 card interrogation" approach to "working a room." This is when you ask each person the same list of questions, as though gathering data for a file card. Instead, follow your genuine interests. Ask open-ended questions and let people talk to you about what interests them most or what is on their mind at the moment.

Third, a good memory. Of course, you may think you do not have a very good memory, but that, too, is a self-image issue, and, in turn, a command to your Servo-Mechanism. Memory can be developed and strengthened by choice. One of the best networkers I know has a terrible memory for names and faces, but is terrific at remembering peoples' "stories"—little details about them. I also once met a U.S. Senator who had an assistant at his elbow throughout the cocktail party. When someone gave him a business card or told him something, he would say "Quite frankly, Bob, I have a terrible memory. But what you've told me is important and I want to follow up on it, so I want Barbara here to jot down the details." I'm not sure there is any one way that is best. But one way or another, and in a way that is flattering to others, you need to capture information about the people you add to your network.

Fourth, a relaxed personality. What do I mean by this? Well, I don't think you are effective if you appear to be trying too hard. We've all heard the person who laughs a bit too loud and too long at every joke, who has the bone-crushing handshake.

The Man Who Wrote the Book on Networking's Best Advice

The man who "wrote the book" on networking is Harvey Mackay. If you do not know who Harvey is, you just haven't been paying attention. He is the owner of an envelope-manufacturing company in Minnesota—hardly a glamorous business—who made himself into a bestselling author largely on the strength of his own networking skills and his giant personal network of contacts. He reveals some of that in his third book on networking, titled *Dig the Well Before You're Thirsty*. Here's what I consider to be Harvey's best advice on networking:

"Network members who call you when they have something that might be an opportunity for you, rather than when they need something from you, are 'A-listers' by definition. By the same token, you'll make a lot more A lists yourself by being proactive on behalf of your network rather than reactive."

Harvey suggests that there is immense power to be had by doing favors for people before they ask. Inevitably, some people will have disappointingly short memories, never display gratitude, and never reciprocate directly. But you cannot let that color your judgement. Overall, Harvey's advice is absolutely certain to pay off.

The title of Harvey's outstanding book *Dig the Well Before You're Thirsty* comes—whether Harvey knows it or not—from Confuscious. It is ancient wisdom. With regard to networking, it means that if you wait to develop your network until you need it, it's too late. So when is the right time in your career to make networking a high priority? Now.

Three Types of Networks You'll Want to Grow and Nurture

Most sales professionals will be well-served by networking within their own company or organization. You need cooperation from people in administration, production, and shipping, from managers, and from other salespeople. From time to time, you'll need a favor. Will someone in shipping push your order out the door ahead of schedule, ahead of others, so you can bail an important customer out of a jam?

Do you know people in every part of your company on a first name basis? Do they know you?

In his book, Harvey Mackay tells the story of Bruce Foraker, who was head of the Bell Telephone Company in New York City, back in the 1920s. A typical "Foraker story" is Harvey's, of Foraker emerging, tuxedo-clad, from a manhole on a cold winter night, at 42nd and Broadway, to the surprise of passers-by. Foraker had come out of the theater, noticed a manhole cover opened and Bell employees working there, so he went over and "dropped in" to visit with them. Foraker was called "the man of 10,000 friends" because his employees held him in such respect.

Today, Herb Kelleher, the CEO of Southwest Airlines, has this kind of reputation. He may appear one day, working with baggage handlers, loading the belly of an aircraft; the next, on a plane, joking with crew and passengers or serving soft drinks and peanuts. Inside the Southwest organization Kelleher has a well-developed, thoroughly nurtured, fine-tuned network of "loyalists" at every level that he can rely on for information when he needs it, for support for a new idea or policy when he wants it.

How's your inside-the-company network? You will find value in developing a network inside your industry. Befriend competitors, top performers, experts. Be known throughout your entire industry for your initiative, healthy curiosity, and willingness to help others.

One of my co-authors is sort of a "center-point" of information flow in his industry. Clients call upon him for advice, opinions, and information frequently. His peers and colleagues call to give him inside information and ask for his opinions or his introductions to important contacts. He says he makes over $100,000 a year just by being alert to the opportunities that surface in this flow of communication.

Develop your broad-based, all-encompassing network that includes your business contacts but also includes doctors, lawyers, Indian chiefs, butchers, bakers, candlestick makers, people in your community, and so on.

But I'm Just Not the Country Club Type

In counseling a salesman, I spent a bit of time asking him about his involvements in civic activities, business groups, and so on—I was evaluating his networking effectiveness. He would have flunked Harvey Mackay's test on networking. When I pressed this issue, he said, "Look, I'm just not the country club type. Getting all dressed up and making small talk with people I don't know well all night isn't for me." I suggested that we dissect and analyze his position.

First, what is the country club type? I told him about some of the people who belonged to my country club. The owner of a pest control firm, that sprayed buildings for bugs. A podiatrist. A veterinarian. A real estate salesperson. Even a retired executive, now driving a limousine, as a chauffeur, to stay active. I said that if we mixed these people in with a crowd on a street corner, he'd be hard-pressed to pick out "the country club types."

"But even if you won't set foot in a club room," I told him, "you can network just about anywhere. There are certainly things you and your wife must enjoy doing, such as antique collecting, ballroom dancing, going to auctions, playing tennis?"

Second, let's tackle "getting all dressed up." Again, there's no law that says you must do your networking in a setting mandating formal attire. There aren't too many tuxedos at the bowling alley or out at your daughter's Little League games. But then again, what's wrong with getting dressed up once in a while and going to a formal affair, the theater, or an art gallery opening? I happen to think it's inspiring to the self-image to put on your "Sunday best" now and then, and hob-nob with classy people in a classy environment. I like the old joke about the guy with his ordinary mutt on a leash at the Westchester dog show. When asked derisively if he had any illusions about the mutt getting a ribbon, he said "No, I just wanted him to meet a better class of dogs." Remember, variety is the spice of life.

Next, "small talk." Quite frankly, I'm not much for "small talk" either. Discussing the price of eggs or the unreliability of the subway is boring to me. I like to talk about "ideas." But I can also be interested in others' travel experiences, hobbies, businesses and occupations, and other interests. And I find it easy to steer conversation into the areas that interest me, just by asking the right questions. This is easily learned; you can do it too.

I suggested to this fellow that he was not "a type" at all. People, I told him, are very complex creatures not to be pigeon-holed as just one type or another. Instead, I urged him to creatively look for a variety of new and different experiences, to expand his horizons and find out whether there were things that interested him that he didn't even know about yet.

I would suggest the same to you. Don't pigeon-hole yourself. Experiment. Why not? What have you got to lose, an evening here or there?

A Final Note About Networking and Zero-Resistance Selling

From a very practical matter, it's this simple: What others say about you is infinitely more credible and persuasive than what you say about you. So, anything you can do to engineer positive comment about you from one person to another pre-empts and eliminates the resistance that most sales professionals face when going in "cold." Networking is the smart way to set up both general, positive word-of-mouth as well as specific referrals, introductions and endorsements.

In addition to this very pragmatic truth about the value of networking, I commend it as a self-image building and strengthening activity. Everything you need to do to be a good networker automatically strengthens and empowers the self-image. Paying attention to others, acquiring new knowledge and information, forming friendships, using your memory, giving of yourself; all these things reinforce a positive, healthy self-image. Further, won't having a growing, thriving, diverse network as an asset enhance your self-confidence? Of course it will!

Chapter 11

Creative Psycho-Cybernetics Mental-Training Exercises

Mental Training Exercise #1

How I've Changed

Spend a week or so adding to the list at left; then complete the list at right, noting those things you now do well that you once did badly.

Things I Did Badly or Failed at as a Kid	Things I Now Do Well or Succeed at as an Adult
_____	_____
_____	_____
_____	_____
_____	_____
_____	_____
_____	_____
_____	_____

Things I Did Badly or Failed at as a Kid	Things I Now Do Well or Succeed at as an Adult
_____	_____
_____	_____
_____	_____
_____	_____
_____	_____
_____	_____
_____	_____
_____	_____
_____	_____
_____	_____
_____	_____

(Reference: Chapter One)

Mental Training Exercise #2

Courage of My Convictions

What are the "positives" I bring to the service of my clients or customers, about myself, integrity, know-how, experience, products, services or my company?

1. _____

2. _____

3. _____

4. _____

5. _____

6. _____

7. _____

8. _____

9. _____

10. _____

11. _____

12. _____

13. _____

14. _____

15. _____

16. _____

17. _____

18. _____

19. _____

20. _____

21. _____

22. _____

23. _____

24. _____

25. _____

26. _____

27. _____

28. _____

29. _____

30. _____

_____

(Reference: Chapter One)

Mental Training Exercise #3

My Greatest Sales Victories

List the times in your sales career when you've been especially creative; sold the tough customer; overcome difficult objections; landed an especially important account, and so on.

1. _____

   _____

   _____

2. _____

   _____

   _____

3. _____

   _____

   _____

4. _____

   _____

   _____

5. _____

_____

_____

6. _____

_____

_____

7. _____

_____

_____

8. _____

_____

_____

_____

(Reference: Chapter One)

Mental Training Exercise #4

Zig Zag

Objections	Answer(s) I Use Now	New Ideas!
1._____	_____	_____
2._____	_____	_____
3._____	_____	_____
4._____	_____	_____
5._____	_____	_____
6._____	_____	_____
7._____	_____	_____
8._____	_____	_____
9._____	_____	_____
10._____	_____	_____
11._____	_____	_____
12._____	_____	_____
13._____	_____	_____
14._____	_____	_____
15._____	_____	_____

(Reference: Chapter Two)

Mental Training Exercise #5

Stature Statements

No, I'm not just another salesman! How I intend to be perceived:

1. _____

_____

_____

2. _____

_____

_____

3. _____

_____

_____

4. _____

_____

_____

5. _____

_____

_____

6. _____

_____

_____

7. _____

_____

_____

8. _____

_____

_____

9. _____

_____

_____

10. _____

_____

_____

_____

(Reference: Chapter Two)

Mental Training Exercise #6

Stature Strategies

Actions I will take to enhance my stature and support my stature statements:

1. _____

_____

_____

2. _____

_____

_____

3. _____

_____

_____

4. _____

_____

_____

5. _____

_____

_____

6. _____

_____

_____

7. _____

_____

_____

8. _____

_____

_____

9. _____

_____

_____

10. _____

_____

_____

(Reference: Chapter Two)

Mental Training Exercise #7

Affirmations

The simplest format for writing affirmations is: "I am the kind of person who _____. (For example, "I am the kind of person who is always on time for appointments and meetings.")

"I am the kind of person who . . .

1. _____

   _____

2. _____

   _____

3. _____

   _____

4. _____

   _____

5. _____

   _____

6. _____

_____

7. _____

_____

8. _____

_____

9. _____

_____

10. _____

_____

(Reference: Chapter Three)

Mental Training Exercise #8

Resiliency Inventory

Times in my life I have been especially resilient:

1. _____

   _____

2. _____

   _____

3. _____

   _____

4. _____

   _____

5. _____

   _____

6. _____

   _____

7. _____

_____

8. _____

_____

9. _____

_____

10. _____

_____

(Reference: Chapter Five)

Mental Training Exercise #9

Message Sent

The message I want to send about my selling career	Actions to take to send the message
1. _____	_____
_____	_____
_____	_____
2. _____	_____
_____	_____
_____	_____
3. _____	_____
_____	_____
_____	_____
4. _____	_____
_____	_____
_____	_____
5. _____	_____
_____	_____
_____	_____

The message I want to send about my selling career	Actions to take to send the message
6. _____	_____
_____	_____
_____	_____
7. _____	_____
_____	_____
_____	_____
8. _____	_____
_____	_____
_____	_____

(Reference: Chapter Seven)

Mental Training Exercise #10

Peace

Here are the Peace of Mind X-Factors I am living, starting now!

1. _____

_____

_____

2. _____

_____

_____

3. _____

_____

_____

4. _____

_____

_____

5. _____

_____

_____

6. _____

_____

_____

7. _____

_____

_____

8. _____

_____

_____

9. _____

_____

_____

10. _____

_____

_____

(Reference: Chapter Seven)

Free Offer from the Foundation

Free Report Reveals Dr. Maxwell Maltz's Most Prized Secrets for "ZERO-RESISTANCE LIVING"

More than 30 Million People have read *Psycho-Cybernetics*, and Dr. Maltz's work with Psycho-Cybernetics has positively influenced countless famous athletes and celebrities, business leaders, top performers in every imaginable field of endeavor for four decades. In this book, you, too, are being introduced to these famous personal achievement enhancing concepts. But this can be just the beginning for you. Dr. Maltz not only proved and publicized the direct relationship between self-image and success, he also developed an entire process of mental training: how to use Creative Psycho-Cybernetics Mental Training Techniques to enjoy Zero-Resistance Living.

What is "Zero-Resistance Living?" It is getting the respect, friendship, recognition, cooperation, joy, financial success and other results you most desire in life *with all resistance removed.* You probably know somebody everybody else calls "lucky." Someone who seems to almost magically get what he or she wants. The person good things come easily to. You can be that person and more. You can experience a whole new type of successful achievement with Zero-Resistance Living!

Who can benefit from Zero-Resistance Living? Everybody. Salespeople, entrepreneurs, executives, investors, negotiators. Parents, spouses, lovers. People desiring to lose weight and keep it off . . . improve their golf games! If there is struggle or difficulty or frustration in ANY aspect of your life, you need to know about Zero-Resistance Living. If you feel you should be advancing faster toward your goals, you need to know about Zero-Resistance Living.

There is *no cost* and no obligation to learn more about the most advanced, complete and practical system for applying Creative Psycho-Cybernetics to achieve very specific results of your choice. At your request, we will send to you, by First Class Mail, a free, confidential report: *Secrets of Zero-Resistance Living.* To request your free report, simply fill in the request form below and drop it in the mail. (If you prefer, fax your name and address and a note requesting the *Zero-Resistance Living Report*, Offer #PH-1, to (602)269-3113 anytime, 24 hours a day, 7 days a week.)

- - - - - - - - - - - - - - - - REQUEST FORM - - - - - - - - - - - - - - - -

Name _____

Mailing Address _____

City, State, Zip _____

Optional:

Phone _____ Fax _____ Business or Occupation _____

Mail to: The Psycho-Cybernetics Foundation, Inc.
5818 N. 7th Street, #103
Phoenix, AZ 85014
(AR#2)

Index